go getter 1

Workbook

Liz Kilbey with Catherine Bright and Jennifer Heath

Contents

1 Label the photos with the names in the box.

Alex ~~Jen~~ Lian Lucas

1 _Jen_   2 _____   3 _____   4 _____

2 Complete the sentences with the words in the box.

~~computers~~ cupcakes Maths skateboarding
Spain twelve

Alex	Jen	Lian	Lucas
12	10	12	🏴
💻	🧁	🛹	♪ $\sqrt[2]{4}$

Hello. My name's Alex.
I love ^{1} _computers_ !

I'm Jen. I'm ten. I love ^{2}
_____ .

Hi. I'm Lian and I'm ^{3} _____ .
My hobby is ^{4} _____ .

My name's Lucas.
I'm from ^{5} _____ .
My hobbies are music
and ^{6} _____ .

3 Complete the words with the letters in the box.

~~e~~ s a h m n

1 _c_ upcake   4 _ pple
2 _ usic   5 _ obby
3 _ port   6 _ ame

4 Put the words in Exercise 3 in alphabetical order.

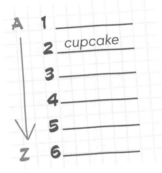

A 1 _____
   2 _cupcake_
   3 _____
   4 _____
   5 _____
Z 6 _____

LOOK!   LL = double L

5 Put the words in the correct order to make sentences.

1 your name What's ?
  What's your name?

2 do your How surname you spell ?
  _____
  _____

3 the UK now I'm in .
  _____
  _____

4 is My hobby music .
  _____
  _____

5 twelve old I'm years .
  _____
  _____

1 Put the words in the correct order to make sentences.

1 Superdug also Dug is .
Dug is also Superdug.

2 is superhero He a .
_____

3 best Kit Dug's friend is .
_____

4 clever She very is .
_____

2 Write the numbers.

five	sixteen	twelve	one	ten
5	☐	☐	☐	☐
eight	four	eleven	seventeen	six
☐	☐	☐	☐	☐
three	twenty	fourteen	eighteen	seven
☐	☐	☐	☐	☐
nineteen	nine	thirteen	two	fifteen
☐	☐	☐	☐	☐

3 Complete the missing numbers.

two four ¹*six* eight ten ² _____ fourteen
³ _____ eighteen ⁴ _____

one three ⁵ _____ seven ⁶ _____ eleven
⁷ _____ fifteen ⁸ _____ nineteen

4 Write the numbers.

1 fifty-seven   *57*   6 nineteen   _____
2 twenty-three   _____   7 thirty   _____
3 seventy-one   _____   8 eighty-six   _____
4 thirteen   _____   9 forty-two   _____
5 sixty-eight   _____   10 a hundred   _____

5 Match colours 1–11 to the words.

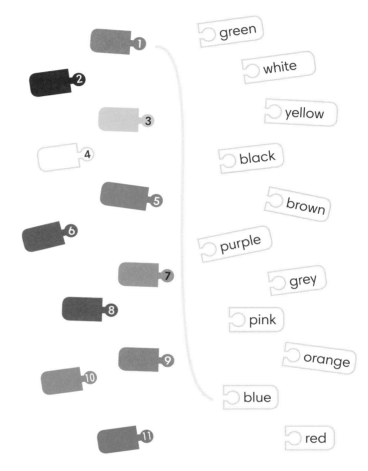

green
white
yellow
black
brown
purple
grey
pink
orange
blue
red

6 Look at the box and write the colours.

eighteen	ninety	thirty	sixteen
fourteen	seventeen	eighty	
nineteen	thirteen	fifty	

1 14   *orange*   6 18 _____
2 30   _____   7 19 _____
3 17   _____   8 16 _____
4 90   _____   9 80 _____
5 13   _____   10 50 _____

1 Circle the correct answer.

1 (pencil sharpener)/
pencil case
2 rubber / pen

3 notebook / ruler
4 pencil / scissors

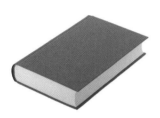

5 book / sandwich
6 coloured pencil /
pencil case

LOOK! a book, a pencil
an apple, an umbrella

2 Circle the correct word.

1 a /(an) apple
4 a / an notebook
2 a / an pencil
5 a / an egg
3 a / an sandwich
6 a / an box

LOOK!
a pencil	six pencils
an orange	two oranges
a box	four boxes
a sandwich	two sandwiches

3 Complete with the plural form of the words in Exercise 2.

1 two _apples_
4 seven _____
2 three _____
5 four _____
3 five _____
6 six _____

4 Find and circle five words in the wordsnake.

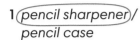

bin desk chair board clock

LOOK! It's a pencil.
They're pencils.

5 Complete with It's or They're.

1 _It's_ a bin.
4 _____ a desk.
2 _____ clocks.
5 _____ chairs.
3 _____ a board.
6 _____ bins.

🔊 2 Classroom language

Close your books.
Listen (to the story).
Look (at the photo).
Open your books.
Read (the text).
Sit down.
Stand up.

Work in pairs.
Write (your name).

Can you help me?
Can you repeat (that)?
I'm ready.
What's *kredka* in English?

LOOK! Can you help me, please?
Stand up, please!

6 Read the expressions. Who usually says them? Circle T (teacher) or S (student).

1 Open your books. (T)/ S
2 Can you help me, please? T / S
3 Stand up. T / S
4 Work in pairs. T / S
5 What's *elefante* in English? T / S
6 Write your name. T / S

7 Put the dialogue in the correct order.

a ☐ Can you repeat that, please?
b ☐ What does *brilliant* mean?
c ☐ It means very good.
d ☐ 1 Hello, Mrs Gold. Can you help me, please
e ☐ Yes, Tom. How can I help?
f ☐ Yes. It means very good.

Vocabulary

1 Circle the correct word.

0 13   (thirteen) / thirty

1 60   sixteen / sixty

2 32   twenty-three / thirty-two

3  blue / green

4 red / yellow

5 black / white

☐/⑤

2 Look at the photos and write the words.

0 _scissors_

1 _____

2 _____

3 _____

4 _____

5 _____

☐/⑤

Grammar

3 Circle the correct answer.

0 It's a / (an) orange.

1 It's / They're pens.

2 It's a / an ruler.

3 It's / They're a coloured pencil.

4 It's a / an elephant.

5 It's an / They're eggs.

☐/⑤

4 Complete with the plural form of the words.

0 eight _pencils_ (pencil)

1 six _____ (orange)

2 two _____ (box)

3 three _____ (bin)

4 two _____ (umbrella)

5 four _____ (rubber)

☐/⑤

Communication

5 Complete the sentences with the words in the box.

> books   down   ~~help~~   pairs   please   up

Can you ⁰_help_ me, ¹_____?

Sit ²_____.

Close your ³_____.

Work in ⁴_____.

Stand ⁵_____.

☐/⑤

Vocabulary ☐/⑩

Grammar ☐/⑩

Communication ☐/⑤

Your total score ▨ / 25

1.1 Vocabulary

1 Who is who in Sally's family? Match a–g to 1–7.

| **LOOK!** | Paul = Mark's father |
| | Lucy = Rose's daughter |

1 ☐ e Sally's father
2 ☐ Sally's mother
3 ☐ Sally's parents
4 ☐ Sally's grandfather
5 ☐ Sally's grandmother
6 ☐ Sally's brother
7 ☐ Sally's sister

2 Match the word fragments to make family words.

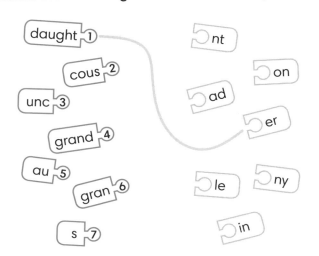

daught ①
cous ②
unc ③
grand ④
au ⑤
gran ⑥
s ⑦

nt
on
ad
er
le
ny
in

3 Look at Mark's family tree. Complete the sentences with one word.

Family tree: Mark; Steven, Holly; Alan + Ruth; David; Helen + Rob; Nick + Mary

1 **Alan:** Nick is my ¹ *father* . He's Mark's ² _____ too.

2 **Holly:** Ruth is my ³ _____ . Steven and I are Mark's ⁴ _____ . I am Helen and Rob's ⁵ _____

3 **Steven:** Holly is my ⁶ _____ . I'm Helen's ⁷ _____ .

I remember that!

4 Read and complete.

1 Amy is Emily's mother.
Emily is Amy's __*daughter*__ .

2 Tom is Danny's father.
Danny is Tom's _____ .

3 Sara is Ben's mother and Ted's aunt.
Ben and Ted are _____ .

4 Ada is Sam's mother. Sam is Rosa's father. Ada is Rosa's _____ .

5 John is David's brother. David is Tina's father. John is Tina's _____ .

to be affirmative

Long form	Short form
I am ten.	I'm ten.
You are ten.	You're ten.
He/She/It is ten.	He/She/It's ten.
We/You/They are ten.	We/You/They're ten.

1 Look at the pictures. Circle the correct word.

A birthday party

1 Look. We *am / (are) / is* at a party.

2 Tom *am / are / is* ten today.

3 I *am / are / is* happy!

A new student

4 He *am / are / is* a teacher.

5 She *am / are / is* a student.

6 They *am / are / is* at school.

7 You *am / are / is* in this class.

Look at Exercise 1. Complete the sentences using short forms of the verb *to be*.

1 Look. We're____ at a party.

2 Tom _____ ten today.

3 I _____ happy!

4 He _____ a teacher.

5 She _____ a student.

6 They _____ at school.

7 You _____ in this class.

3 Complete the dialogue with *am*, *are* or *is*.

Harry: Hi. I ¹ _am_ Harry.

Jack: Hi, Harry. I ² _____ Jack. You ³ _____ in Class 2 with me. Welcome!

Harry: Thanks.

Jack: This is Tony. He ⁴ _____ my classmate. We ⁵ _____ best friends too. Mrs Lee and Mr Brown ⁶ _____ my favourite teachers.

LOOK!

I	→	my	It's **my** birthday. **I'm** ten!
you	→	your	It's **your** birthday. **You're** eleven!
she	→	her	It's **her** birthday. **She's** nine.
he	→	his	It's **his** birthday. **He's** twelve.

4 Complete with *my*, *your*, *his* or *her*.

This is ¹ _my_ brother. ² _____ name is Alex. The present is for granny. ³ _____ name is Sophie.

This is ⁴ _____ present, Granny.

★ 5 Complete the text with the words in the box.

~~am~~ are Her is my They

Hi! I ¹ _am_ Tom. This is ² _____ family. My parents' names ³ _____ Amy and Andrew. ⁴ _____ are teachers. My sister ⁵ _____ thirteen. ⁶ _____ name is Katie.

Extra Online Practice

Unit 1, Video and Grammar

9

to be negative

Long form	Short form
I am not Spanish.	I'm not Spanish.
You are not Spanish.	You aren't Spanish.
He/She/It is not Spanish.	He/She/It isn't Spanish.
We/You/They are not Spanish.	We/You/They aren't Spanish.

1 Rewrite the sentences using short forms of the verb to be.

1 My friends are not at home.
   My friends aren't at home.

2 You are not right.
   _____

3 I am not a superhero.
   _____

4 Ben is not my friend.
   _____

5 She is not my aunt.
   _____

6 They are not my cousins.
   _____

2 Write negative sentences. Use the short form of the verb to be.

1 She's eleven.
   She's at school.
   She _isn't eleven_ .
   She _____ .

2 They're happy.
   They're at home.
   They _____ .
   _____
   _____

3 He's a teacher.
   He's ready for school.
   He _____ .
   _____
   _____

3 Vocabulary Complete the words and write the nationalities.

1 P _o_ _l_ _a_ _n_ d   _Polish_

2 F _ _ _ _ _ e   _____

3 the _ _   _____

4 I _ _ _ y   _____

5 C _ _ _ _ a   _____

6 the _ _ _   _____

7 S _ _ _ n   _____

4 Write sentences that are true for you. Write am, 'm not, are, aren't, is or isn't.

1 My school _____ in the USA.
2 My English teacher _____ British.
3 My friends _____ in China.
4 My parents _____ Polish.
5 I _____ Italian.
6 I _____ ten.

✳ 5 Complete the dialogue with the verb to be. Use an affirmative form (✔) or a negative form (✗).

Kit: It ¹ _is_ (✔) you, Dug! You ² _____ (
    with your granddad and granny, right

Dug: No, I ³ _____ (✗). They ⁴ _____ (✔) my
    parents. My dad ⁵ _____ (✔) British, b
    my mother ⁶ _____ (✗) British. She
    ⁷ _____ (✔) Polish.

Kit: It ⁸ _____ (✗) a new photo.

Dug: That's right. The photo ⁹ _____ (✔) ve
    old.

3 Introductions

A: *Mum*, this is *Lucas*.
He is my *friend/classmate*.
Lucas, this is my *mum*.
B: Hello, *Lucas*. Nice to meet you.
C: Nice to meet you too.

1 Complete the dialogues.

Hi, Jill.

1 a Sorry, Mum!
  b Hi, Mum!
  c It's OK, Mum!
2 a This is Amy.
  b I'm Amy.
  c You are here, Amy.

Amy is my new classmate.

3 a You're Amy.
  b Hello, Amy.
  c Thank you, Amy.
4 a Nice to meet you, Jill.
  b Nice to meet you, Mrs Wilson.
  c Nice to meet you, Amy.

2 Complete the dialogue with the words in the box.

He's   Hi   Nice   ~~this is~~   to meet you

Thomas: Hi, Stella, ¹ _this is_ Frankie. ² _____
my cousin.
Stella: ³ _____ , Frankie. Nice ⁴ _____ .
Frankie: ⁵ _____ to meet you too Stella.

3 Complete the dialogue with sentences a–d.

May: ¹ _b_
Auntie Sue: Oh, hello, May!
May: And this is Nancy. ² ___
Auntie Sue: Hello, Nancy. ³ ___
Nancy: Hello, Mrs Smith. ⁴ ___

a She's my best friend at school.
b Hi, Auntie Sue.
c Nice to meet you.
d Nice to meet you too.

4 Write a dialogue like in Exercise 3. Introduce your English friend to your teacher.

You: _____
Teacher: _____
You: _____

Your friend: _____
Teacher: _____

Extra Online Practice

Unit 1, Video and Communication

11

My photo album

1 ☐

In this photo, my mum and dad are with Aunt Ellie. They aren't at home, they're on holiday in Spain. They are happy. Aunt Ellie is my dad's sister. My dad and his family are Spanish.

2 ☐

This is my friend, Bea. She's in the garden. Her mum is Italian and her dad is British. She's fun. Sweep is in the photo too. He's Bea's dog.

3 ☐

Hi. I'm Silvia and this is my brother, Nick. I'm twelve and he's nine. We're from Manchester. It's in the UK.

---

1 Read the texts. Match texts 1–3 to photos A–C.

2 Read the texts again. Match 1–6 to a–f.

1	c	Hi. My name's	a my aunt.
2	☐	I'm	b my friend.
3	☐	My brother is	c Silvia.
4	☐	Ellie is	d 12.
5	☐	Bea is	e a dog.
6	☐	Sweep is	f 9.

3 Complete the sentences with British, Italian or Spanish. Check your answers in the texts.

1 Silvia is ___British___ .
2 Nick is _____ .
3 Silvia's dad is _____ .
4 Aunt Ellie is _____ .
5 Bea's mother is _____ .
6 Bea's father is _____ .

4 Vocabulary **Look at the photos and complete the words.**

1 I'm at a p _ _ _ _ today.

2 We aren't at s _ _ _ _ _ today.

3 My sister and my mother are in the g _ _ _ _ _ .

4 My granny and my grand[...] are in the p _ _ _ .

1  🔊 4 Read and listen. Circle T (true) or F (false).

1 Rob and Victor are best friends. (T)/ F
2 They're at Rob's house. T / F
3 Rob's mum and Victor's mum are best friends. T / F

4 Rob's on holiday. T / F
5 Rob and Mel are in the UK. T / F
6 Rob and Mel are cousins. T / F

🔊 4 Listen again. Complete the tables.

Rob

Age: _____10_____
Nationality: _____

Victor

Age: _____
Nationality: _____

Mel

Age: _____
Nationality: _____

Capital letters

Use a capital letter for names of people, countries and nationalities.
Use a capital letter for the pronoun *I* and at the beginning of every sentence too.

My best friend is Jack.   I'm from France.
Giorgia and Toni are Italian.

3 Correct the text. Add capital letters.

Clara
~~clara~~ and bianca are best friends.
clara is nine and bianca is ten. clara
is from the UK. she's british. bianca
is from italy. she's italian.

4 Read the text in Exercise 3 again. Complete the table.

	Clara	Bianca
Age	9	
Country		
Nationality		

5 Look at the information and write about Pierre and Pedro.

	Pierre	Pedro
Age	12	11
Country	France	Spain
Nationality	French	Spanish

Pierre and Pedro are best friends.
Pierre is
_____
_____
_____
_____
_____

Vocabulary

1 Complete the pairs.

0 mum and *dad*

1 _____ and uncle

2 mother and _____

3 _____ and sister

4 son and _____

5 _____ and grandad

☐/⑤

2 Look and complete the words.

0 She's from **P** *o l a n d*.   1 He's in the **g** _ _ _ _ _ .

2 She's **A** _ _ _ _ _ _ _ .   3 They are at **s** _ _ _ _ _ .

4 Paris is in **F** _ _ _ _ _ .   5 She's at **h** _ _ _ .

☐/⑤

Grammar

3 Complete the sentences with the verb *to be*. Use an affirmative form (✔) or a negative form (✗).

0 This ___*isn't*___ (✗) my garden. It's a park!

1 My best friends _____ (✔) Maya and Jane.

2 Maya _____ (✔) Italian.

3 Jane and I _____ (✗) Italian.

4 We _____ (✔) from the UK.

5 I _____ (✗) in the UK in this photo!

☐/⑤

4 Circle the correct answer.

This is Jack, and this is ⁰*Jack /* (Jack's) cousin. ¹*His / Her* name is Freddie. They are with ²*Freddie / Freddie's* dog, Wolfie.

This is Clara, and this is ³*his / her* best friend, Nadia. ⁴*Nadia / Nadia's* mum and ⁵*Clara / Clara's* mum are best friends too.

☐/⑤

Communication

5 Complete the dialogue with one word in each gap.

A: Jack, ⁰ *this* ¹_____ my friend, Harry.

B: ²_____ , Harry. ³_____ to meet you.

C: Hi, Jack. Nice to ⁴_____ you ⁵_____ .

☐/⑤

Vocabulary	☐/⑩
Grammar	☐/⑩
Communication	☐/⑤
Your total score	/ 25

Extra Online Practice

Unit 1, Language Revision

14

Word blog: Family and friends

1 My photos Look and complete.

1 my mum's brother
= my _ _ _ _ _

2 my parents' daughter
= my _ _ _ _ _ _

3 my dad's mum
= my _ _ _ _ _ _

4 my aunt's sons
= my _ _ _ _ _ _ _

2 My quiz Match 1–6 to a–f.

 1   Say *Cześć!*   a in Chinese.

 2   Say *Bonjour!*   b in Italian.

 3   Say *Ciao!*   c in English.

 4   Say *¡Hola!*   d in Polish.

 5   Say *Hello!*   e in French.

 6   Say *Nihao!*   f in Spanish.

3 Get more Find and circle four birthday words. Label the pictures with them.

awpartykzepresentjouballoonubcake

1 _____   2 _____   3 _____   4 _____

Get more words

Happy birthday!

Match sentences 1–12 to photos A–D. There are two extra sentences.

1   C   This is my brother, Josh.
2   He's at school.
3   This is my cousin. She's ten.
4   She isn't happy in the photo.
5   She's in the park.
6   Mr Thomson is 30.
7   This is my granny.
8   He's at home.
9   She's my mum's mother.
10   He's 75.
11   He's my teacher.
12   She's 60 years old.

A

B

D

C

Fun Spot

15

2.1 Vocabulary

Clothes for kids

1 *trainers*
2 _____
3 _____
4 _____
5 _____
6 _____

1 Label photos 1–6 with the words in the box.

dress   hoodie   jeans
jumper   skirt   ~~trainers~~

2 Find and circle nine clothes words. Then complete the words.

T	T	R	A	C	K	S	U	I	T
E	H	B	W	Q	L	W	T	F	D
L	T	V	I	H	S	H	O	E	S
R	R	B	U	E	S	Y	P	U	S
Y	O	I	Y	R	C	L	T	B	H
B	U	T	F	F	A	E	U	X	I
O	S	M	V	C	P	C	G	Q	R
O	E	I	J	A	C	K	E	T	T
T	R	M	Q	W	S	N	Q	D	P
S	S	C	O	A	T	F	I	S	Y

1 t*racksui*t   4 j____t   7 t____p
2 t____s   5 s____s   8 s____t
3 b____s   6 c____p   9 c____t

LOOK! The T-shirt is blue.
The shoes are brown.
The jeans are blue.

3 Complete the sentences. Use the words in Exercises 1 and 2.

1 Her *jacket* is grey.   5 His _____ is blue
2 Her _____ is pink.   6 His _____ is gree
3 Her _____ are blue.   7 His _____ are bl
4 Her _____ are brown.   8 His _____ are wh

I rememb
that!

4 What are they? Label photos 1–6.

1 *cap*
2 _____
3 _____

4 _____
5 _____
6 _____

this, that, these, those

→	→
This is Jen's top.	That is Alex's T-shirt
This top is Jen's.	That T-shirt is Alex's.
These are Jen's trainers.	Those are Alex's trainers.
These trainers are Jen's.	Those trainers are Alex's.

1 Complete the sentences with *This*, *That*, *These* or *Those*.

1 _That_ is Alex's bag.   2 _____ is Dad's bag.

3 _____ shoes are Mum's.   4 _____ shoes are Jen's.

5 _____ dress is Jen's.   6 _____ is Mum's dress.

2 Vocabulary Label the pictures with the words in the box.

big	~~boring~~	cool	long	new	old
short	small				

1 _boring_ and _____   2 _____ and _____

3 _____ and _____   4 _____ and _____

LOOK! Her boots are too big!
His shirt is too small!

3 Complete the sentences with *is/are too* and adjectives in Exercise 2.

1 His cap _is too small_ .
2 His jeans _____.
3 His T-shirt _____.
4 His trainers _____.

⁎ 4 Look at the photos and write sentences. Use the words in the box and *this*, *that*, *these* or *those*.

an old boot	new trousers	boring shoes
~~a cool cap~~	a small shirt	

1 _This is a cool cap._
2 _____
3 _____
4 _____
5 _____

Extra Online Practice

 Unit 2, Video and Grammar

2.3 Grammar

to be questions and short answers

?	Short form
Am I OK?	Yes, I am. / No, I'm not.
Are you OK?	Yes, you are. / No, you aren't.
Is he/she/it OK?	Yes, he/she/it is. / No, he/she/it isn't.
Are you/we/they OK?	Yes, you/we/they are. / No, you/we/they aren't.
What is it?	It's my new suit.

1 Add a question mark (?) or a full stop (.).

1 Is he French [?]
2 My brother is eight years old [ ]
3 Are you a student [ ]
4 Is Lee your friend [ ]
5 I'm cool [ ]
6 Are they happy [ ]

2 Complete the questions with *Is* or *Are*.

1 __Is__ Kit a cat?
2 _____ she black?
3 _____ Kit and Dug friends?
4 _____ they at school?
5 _____ Dug's suit blue and red?
6 _____ his suit too small?

3 Match answers a–f to the questions in Exercise 2.

a [ ] Yes, it is.   d [ ] No, it isn't.
b [ ] Yes, they are.   e [ ] No, they aren't.
c [1] Yes, she is.   f [ ] No, she isn't.

4 Think about Dug and Kit. Complete the answers with your own ideas.

1 Are Dug and Kit cool? _____ , they _____ .
2 Is he clever? _____ , he _____ .
3 Is she a good friend? _____ , she _____ .
4 Is the suit OK? _____ , it _____ .
5 Are you a superhero? _____ , I _____ .

5 Complete the dialogue. Use *am/are/is* and the words in brackets.

A: ¹ _Are you_ (you) May?
B: Yes, ² _____ .
A: ³ _____ (Ben) your brother?
B: No, ⁴ _____ . He's my classmate.
A: ⁵ _____ (you) best friends?
B: Yes, ⁶ _____ .
A: ⁷ _____ (he) Spanish?
B: Yes, ⁸ _____ . He's from Barcelona.

✱ 6 Put the words in the correct order to make questions.

1 is What name your ?
   What is your name?
2 at Are school you ?
   _____
3 eleven you Are ?
   _____
4 your best ten friend Is ?
   _____
5 best name What friend's is your ?
   _____
6 friends your happy Are ?
   _____

✱ 7 Answer the questions in Exercise 6 for you.

1 _My name ..._
2 _____
3 _____
4 _____
5 _____
6 _____

5 Asking for personal information

What's your name?
How old are you?
Where are you from?
What's your favourite *music/sport/film*?
Who's your favourite *actor/singer/ sports person*?

Complete the dialogue with sentences a–e.

Man: Hi. Welcome to the show. ¹ _e_
Nancy: My name's Nancy.
Man: Where are you from?
Nancy: ² _____
Man: ³ _____
Nancy: I'm eleven.
Man: What's your favourite sport?
Nancy: ⁴ _____
Man: Who's your favourite actor?
Nancy: ⁵ _____

a Swimming. I love it.
b London, England.
c Asa Butterfield.
d How old are you?
e What's your name?

2 Circle the correct answer.

1 (*What*) / *Who* is your name?
2 *What* / *Where* are you from?
3 *How* / *Where* old are you?
4 *Who* / *Where* is your favourite sports person?
5 *What* / *Who* is your favourite film?

3 Match answers a–e to the questions in Exercise 2.

a ☐ Manchester, England.
b [1] I'm Danny.
c ☐ Renato Sanches. He's from Portugal.
d ☐ *The Incredibles.*
e ☐ Ten.

4 Read. Then complete the questions for Emma.

by Ben Carter
Welcome, Emma!

Emma is new to our school. She's ¹ten, and she's ²from Cardiff, Wales. Her favourite sport is ³tennis, and her favourite book is ⁴*The Hobbit*. Her favourite singer is ⁵Alicia Keys.

Welcome to our school, Emma!

1 How old ___ *are you* ___ ?
2 Where _____ ?
3 What _____ ?
4 What _____ ?
5 Who _____ ?

5 Answer the questions in Exercise 4 for you.

1 *I'm ...* _____
2 _____
3 _____
4 _____
5 _____

Extra Online Practice

Unit 2, Video and Communication

Our Clever Clothes!

1 ☐ Hi, I'm Sam. Look at this – it's a cool hoodie, but that's not all. It's an MP3 player too, with my favourite music. My hoodie is green and my sister Anna's is purple.

A

2 ☐ My name's Becky. These jeans are my favourite clothes. They're cool and they're clever too. Look. This is a pocket for my mobile phone. It's a phone charger too. My jeans are fantastic!

B

3 ☐ Hello. I'm Luke. These trainers are my favourite things. They're red and yellow and they're very cool. Look – what are these? They're small wheels! My trainers are skates too! I love my clever trainers.

C

1 Read the text. Match children 1–3 to their clothes A–C.

2 Read the texts again. Who is it? Choose from the box. There is one extra name.

Anna   Becky   Luke   Sam

1 *My favourite things are red and yellow. I'm _____ .*

2 *I'm Sam's sister. I'm _____ .*

3 *My best clothes are my jeans. I'm _____ .*

3 **Vocabulary** Look at the picture. What can you see? Circle T (true) or F (false).

1 mountain bike	T /Ⓕ		4 games console	T / F
2 backpack	T / F		5 mobile phone	T / F
3 laptop computer	T / F		6 skateboard	T / F

Label the pictures with the words in the box.

> backpack   games console
> hoodie   mobile phone
> mountain bike   trainers

1 ☐ _trainers_   2 ☐ _____

3 ☐ _____   4 ☐ _____

5 ☐ _____   6 ☐ _____

🔊 6 Listen to Luke and Rosa. What do they talk about? Tick (✔) the pictures in Exercise 1.

🔊 6 Listen again. Circle the correct answer.

1 Luke's _____ is new.

a    b

2 Rosa's favourite colour is _____ .

a   b

3 Luke's trainers are _____ .

a new   b _old_

4 Rosa's favourite thing is her _____ .

a   b

Punctuation

Remember to use punctuation marks!
What are your favourite things?
They're my backpack, my phone and my computer.
They are cool!

4 Correct Harry's blog post. Add punctuation marks.

> ,   .   ?   !

Harry's blog

Hi ¹☐!☐
My name is Harry ²☐ My favourite things are my school bag ³☐ my mobile phone and my skateboard ⁴☐ What's my favourite colour ⁵☐ That's easy ⁶☐ It's orange ⁷☐

5 Now write a blog post about you. Use punctuation marks.

Hello/Hi!   _____

name?   _____
_____

favourite things?   _____
_____

favourite colour?   _____
_____

Vocabulary

1 Circle the odd one out.

0 (T-shirt) boots shoes
1 cool fantastic boring
2 backpack top dress
3 trousers jeans cap
4 long big top
5 jacket skirt coat

☐/⑤

2 Look at the photo and write the words.

0	*cap*	3	_____
1	_____	4	_____
2	_____	5	_____

☐/⑤

Grammar

3 Circle the correct answer.

0 My shoes _____ too small.
  a is
  (b) are

1 _____ T-shirt isn't big.
  a This
  b These

2 What _____ it?
  a are
  b is

3 _____ are my brother
  a That
  b Those

4 Her boots _____ cool
  a are
  b is

5 _____ they your book
  a Is
  b Are

☐/

4 Answer yes (✔) or no (✗). Use short answers.

0 A: Are you OK?
  B: ✔ *Yes, I am.*

1 A: Is it your backpack?
  B: ✔ _____

2 A: Are your new shoes black?
  B: ✗ _____

3 A: Are we friends?
  B: ✔ _____

4 A: Is Tom your brother
  B: ✗ _____

5 A: Is Ella at school?
  B: ✔ _____

☐/

Communication

5 Put the sentences in the dialogue in the correct order.

a ☐ Eleven. Are you 11 too?
b ☐ Harry Potter, Book One.
c [0] Hello, I'm Benjamin. What's your name?
d ☐ Hi. I'm Jackie. I'm from England. Where are you from?
e ☐ I'm from England too. How old are you?
f ☐ No, I'm not. I'm 12. What's your favourite book?

☐/

Vocabulary	☐/⑩
Grammar	☐/⑩
Communication	☐/⑤
Your total score	☐/25

Extra Online Practice

Unit 2, Language Revision

Word blog: My things

1 My photos Circle the correct word.

1 hoodie / top   2 skirt / dress   3 boots / trainers

2 Get more Match the word fragments to make four words and label the pictures.

guitar   hero
sing   ist
act   super   er   or

1 _____   2 _____   3 _____   4 _____

3 My chat room Complete the conversation.

Hi. Look at my new
1 _____ 📱 .

Cool! And is that a new
2 _____ 🎒 too?

No, it isn't. It's my sister's. It's very big because her clothes are in it: her ³ _____ 👜 , her ⁴ _____ 👕 and her ⁵ _____ 🧢 .

Get more words

Fantastic!

Concert

Find and circle things that are different. In your notebook, write eight sentences.

Fun Spot

A

£99

B

£99

In Picture A, the dog is small. In Picture B, it is …

Reading and Writing

1 Read the text. What is it about? Circle the correct answer.

  a Birthday presents.
  b A birthday party.

☐/①

2 Read the text again. Complete the sentences with one word in each gap.

0 It's _Jade's_ birthday party.
1 Jade's birthday _____ is pink.
2 All her _____ and family are at the party.
3 Jade's grandad _____ English.
4 Jade's presents _____ very cool.
5 Her favourite present is her _____ mobile phone.
6 In the photo Jade is in her new red _____ .

☐/⑥

3 Look and read. Write *yes* or *no*.

0 Granny's dog is in the picture. _no_
00 The boy's cap is too big. _yes_
1 They are in the garden. _____
2 Dad's trousers are too long. _____
3 Mum's shoes are red. _____
4 The boy's hoodie is green. _____
5 Granny's mobile phone is old. _____

☐/⑤

BLOG

Jade is my best friend. This is a photo of her birthday party. Look at her cake! She's twelve. She's very happy.

The party is at Jade's house. All her friend and family are there but they aren't in the photo. Her granny and grandad are there Her grandad isn't English. He's from China

Her presents are very cool. Her favourite present is her new mobile phone. It's blue, her favourite colour. She's in her new red t in the photo.

I love birthday parties!

4 Complete five sentences about Emily. Use *is*, *is from* or *are* and the information in the table.

0 Name	Emily
1 Country	the UK
2 Brother	11
3 Best friend	Katia
4 Favourite colours	purple and wh
5 Favourite thing	her jacket

0 This _is Emily_ .
1 She _____
2 Her brother _____
3 Her best friend's name _____
4 Emily's favourite colours _____
_____
5 Her favourite thing _____

☐/

Listening

5 🔊 7 Listen and tick (✔) the correct answer.

0 Where is Uncle Tom?

A ☐ B ✔ C ☐

1 What's Lily's favourite birthday present?

A ☐ B ☐ C ☐

2 What's in the bag?

A ☐ B ☐ C ☐

3 How old is Jo?

A ☐ B ☐ C ☐

4 Which is Mrs Smith's dog?

A ☐ B ☐ C ☐

☐/④

Communication

6 John is a new student in May's class. Match May's questions 0–4 to John's answers a–f. There is one extra answer.

0 [c] What's your name?
1 ☐ How old are you?
2 ☐ Where are you from?
3 ☐ What's your favourite sport?
4 ☐ Who's your favourite singer?

a It's football.
b Beyoncé.
c It's John.
d British.
e The UK.
f I'm thirteen.

☐/④

Reading and Writing ☐/⑰
Listening ☐/④
Communication ☐/④
Your total score ☐/ 25

3 In the house

3.1 Vocabulary

1 Look at the pictures. Circle the correct answer.

1 It's *a wall /* (*a door*).
2 It's *an armchair / a desk.*
3 It's *a floor / a sofa.*
4 It's *a bed / a chair.*
5 It's *a wardrobe / a table.*
6 It's *a fridge / a door.*
7 It's *a window / a wall.*

2 Complete the sentences.

1 It's a ___*bath*___ .

2 It's a _____ .

3 It's a _____ .

4 It's a _____ .

5 It's a _____ .

6 It's a _____ .

3 Where are these objects from? Label the rooms with the words in the box.

> bathroom   bedroom   garage   garden
> ~~kitchen~~   living room

1   *kitchen*

2 _____

3 _____

4 _____

5 _____

6 _____

4 Where are they? Match 1–5 to a–e.

I rememb that!

1 [e] milk and eggs
2 [ ] notebooks and pencils
3 [ ] jumpers and trousers
4 [ ] a sofa and armchairs
5 [ ] a car and bikes

a in the wardrobe
b in the garage
c on the desk
d in the living room
e in the fridge

there is / there are affirmative

➕ There's (There is) a phone on the sofa.

There are two DVDs behind the sofa.

There are some sweets under the sofa.

1 Circle the correct answer. Find the correct picture. Write A or B.

1 *There is* / *There are* an armchair. ☐ B
2 *There is* / *There are* five chairs. ☐
3 *There is* / *There are* a small picture. ☐
4 *There is* / *There are* a bed. ☐
5 *There is* / *There are* two sofas. ☐
6 *There is* / *There are* four windows. ☐

(A)

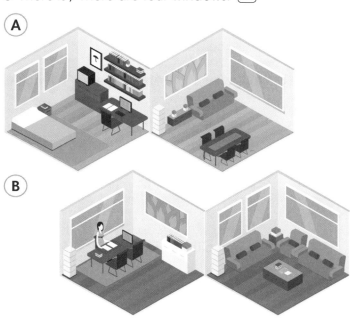

(B)

Vocabulary Complete the sentences with *in, on, in front of, behind, under* or *next to*.

1 Alex and Lian are ___*in*___ the living room.
2 There are two tables _____ the sofa.
3 There's a mobile phone _____ the black table.
4 There are trainers _____ the white table. Yuck!
5 Lian is _____ the sofa.
6 There's a school bag _____ Lian.

3 Look and circle the correct answers.

1 There *is* / *are* two trees *in* / *on* the garden.
2 There *is* / *are* a cat *on* / *under* the car.
3 There *is* / *are* two girls *in front of* / *behind* the door.
4 There *is* / *are* a wall *behind* / *on* the garden.
5 There *is* / *are* a garage *in front of* / *next to* the house.

✸ **4 Complete the sentences with one word in each gap.**

1 There ¹___*are*___ blue walls ²_____ my bedroom. There ³_____ pictures of my family and friends ⁴_____ the walls.
2 There's ⁵_____ small table ⁶_____ to my bed. There ⁷_____ some books and a laptop on the table. ⁸_____ are some notebooks too.

✸ **5 Write four sentences about your bedroom. Use the words in the box and prepositions of place.**

| bed   desk   door   window   chair |
| photos   wardrobe   books   box |

1 _____
_____
2 _____
_____
3 _____
_____
4 _____
_____

Extra Online Practice

Unit 3, Video and Grammar

there is / there are
negative and questions

━	There isn't a blue car.	There aren't any people.
?	Is there a blue car?	Are there any people?
	Yes, there is. / No, there isn't.	Yes, there are. / No, there aren't.

1 Circle the correct answer.

1 There *isn't* / *aren't* any chairs in the kitchen.
2 *Is* / *Are* there any laptops in the classroom?
3 *Is* / *Are* there a cat in the garden?
4 There *isn't* / *aren't* a TV in the living room.
5 *Is* / *Are* there a number on the door?
6 There *isn't* / *aren't* any people in the park.

> **LOOK!**
> There isn't a tree. Is there a tree?
> There aren't any trees. Are there any trees?

2 Put the words in the correct order to make sentences. Look at the picture and circle T (true) or F (false).

1 the There isn't living room a table in .
   There isn't a table in the living room.   T / **F**
2 There table a phone on isn't the .
   _____   T / F
3 room isn't There the a TV in .
   _____   T / F
4 parrots There in any the aren't picture .
   _____   T / F
5 the books aren't any There picture in .
   _____   T / F

3 Complete the questions with *Is there a* or *Are there any*.

1 *Is there a* laptop in the bedroom?
2 _____ photos on your laptop?
3 _____ cat under the bed?
4 _____ clothes in that bag?
5 _____ bike in the garage?
6 _____ apples on the tree?

4 Match answers a–f to the questions in Exercise 3.

a ☐ No, there aren't. It's a new laptop.
b ☐ Yes, there are. My new jeans and a T-shirt.
c ☐ Yes, there is. There's a blue mountain b[...]
d ☐ No, there aren't. It isn't an apple tree[...]
e ☐ 1 Yes, there is. It's on the desk.
f ☐ No, there isn't. But there are two cats [...] the wardrobe!

✷5 Write questions. Answer yes (✔) or no (✗). Use short answers.

1 trees / in your garden?
   A: *Are there any trees in your garden?*
   B: ✗ *No, there aren't.*
2 a garage / next to your house?
   A: _____
   B: ✗ _____
3 armchairs / in your living room?
   A: _____
   B: ✔ _____ Two armchairs and a sofa.
4 pencils / on your desk?
   A: _____
   B: ✗ _____ They're in my b[...]
5 a desk / in your bedroom?
   A: _____
   B: ✔ _____ It's in front of t[...] window.

✷6 Complete the text with one word in each gap.

There ¹ *are* a lot of things in the garage[...]
There's ² _____ old fridge and there ³ ___
two old armchairs. Are there ⁴ _____ bike[...]
No, there ⁵ _____ and there isn't ⁶ _____ c[...]

🔊 8 **Having a guest**

A: Hello. Please, come in.
B: Thank you.
A: Would you like a *sandwich*?
B: Yes, please. / No, thank you.

A: Where's the *bathroom*, please?
B: It's *upstairs/downstairs*.
   It's *next to* the *living room*.
   Let me show you.

Complete the dialogues.

a It's in the living room. Let me show you.
b Would you like an apple?
c Hi. Come in!
d Where's your laptop?
e Yes, please!
f Thanks.

2 Read the dialogues and circle TWO correct answers.

1 A: Where's the bathroom?
   B: _____
   ⓐ It's upstairs.
   ⓑ Let me show you.
   c Yes, there is.

2 A: Would you like a biscuit?
   B: _____
   a No, thanks.
   b Let's go to the kitchen.
   c Yes, please.

3 A: Where's my coat?
   B: _____
   a Here you are.
   b It's on the chair.
   c Come in.

4 A: Please, come in. Would you like a cupcake?
   B: _____
   a Yes, I'm hungry.
   b There's a cupcake.
   c No, thank you.

5 A: Where's your bike?
   B: _____
   a No, it isn't.
   b In the garden.
   c At my friend's house.

3 Complete the dialogues with one word in each gap.

1 *Hello. ¹Please come in.*
   ² _____ you.

3 *Would you ³ _____ a biscuit?*
   ⁴ _____ , please. Yum!

2 *⁵ _____ 's the bathroom, please?*
   It's upstairs. Let me ⁶ _____ you.

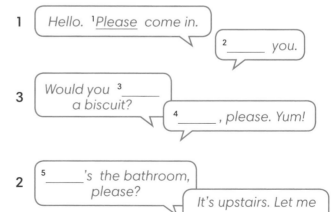

Extra Online Practice

Unit 3, Video and Communication

A house in a tree!

**Luke is on holiday.
Look! His holiday house is in a tree!**

Yes, we're in a tree house! It's very cool. There are two bedrooms: one is big and one is small. In the small bedroom there's a desk and a chair and there are two beds – for me and my brother. The big bedroom is for my mum and dad. There's a small bathroom too.

There's a big kitchen and there's a small living room too. There's a table in the kitchen and there are four chairs. There's a fridge too. In the living room there's a long sofa in front of a big window. There isn't a TV but that's OK.

1 What is there in the tree house? Read and tick (✔).

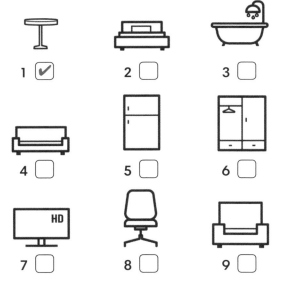

1 ✔　　2 ☐　　3 ☐

4 ☐　　5 ☐　　6 ☐

7 ☐　　8 ☐　　9 ☐

2 Complete the sentences with one number in each gap.

1 There are _____ rooms in the house.
2 There are _____ big rooms.
3 There are _____ people in Luke's family.

3 **Vocabulary** Complete the puzzle.

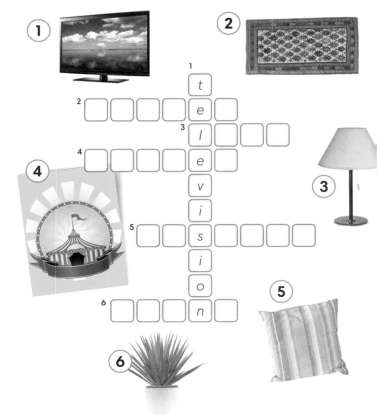

```
          1
          t
2 ☐☐☐☐☐ e ☐
          3
          l ☐☐☐
4 ☐☐☐☐☐ e ☐
          v
          i
        5 s ☐☐☐☐☐☐
          i
          o
6 ☐☐☐☐ n
```

1 🔊 9 **Listen to the dialogue. What's it about? Circle the correct answer.**

a Nancy's new house

b Nancy's bedroom

c Nancy's family

2 🔊 9 **Listen again. Correct the sentences.**

1 In Nancy's house there are five rooms.

_____

2 The bathroom is upstairs.

_____

3 There are two bedrooms.

_____

4 There's a TV in Nancy's bedroom.

_____

3 🔊 9 **Listen again. Tick (✔) Nancy's house.**

(A) ☐

(B) ☐

(C) ☐

Apostrophes

Remember to use apostrophes with contractions.

there is = there's   is not = isn't   are not = aren't

it is = it's   they are = they're   that is = that's

4 Correct Jack's text. Add apostrophes.

My dream bedroom

by Jack

In my dream bedroom <u>there's</u> a big bed. Its blue. Next to the bed theres a table with a lamp. On the floor theres a big carpet. Its red, yellow and orange. There arent any plants in the room but there are lots of posters and photos of my friends. There isnt a TV but theres a computer.

5 Now write about your dream bedroom. Use the words in the box or your own ideas.

> TV   computer   games console   books
> carpet   cushions   lamp   posters
> bed   desk   table   sofa   fridge

_____

_____

_____

_____

_____

_____

_____

_____

_____

_____

_____

Vocabulary

1 Look at the photos and the letters. Label the photos.

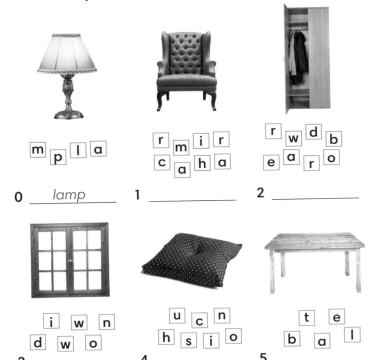

m p l a

0 ___lamp___   1 _____   2 _____

3 _____   4 _____   5 _____

◯/⑤

2 Look at the pictures. Circle the correct answer.

The mouse is ⁰ *in* / on the ¹*bathroom* / *bedroom*.
It's ²*under* / *on* the desk.

This is the ³*kitchen* / *living room*. The mouse is
⁴*in* / *in front of* the ⁵*fridge* / *door*.

◯/⑤

Grammar

3 Circle the correct answer.

0 There *isn't* / *aren't* a cat in the garden.

1 There *is* / *are* three books on the desk.

2 There isn't *a pen* / *any pens* in my bag.

3 There *isn't* / *aren't* any chairs in the classroom.

4 There *is* / *are* a book on the desk.

5 There *are* / *aren't* any plants in the living room.

◯/⑤

4 Complete the dialogues with one word in each gap.

1 A: ⁰ ___Is___ there a television in the kitcher

B: No, there ¹_____ .

2 A: ²_____ there ³_____ coats in the wardrobe?

B: No, there ⁴_____ .

3 A: Is there ⁵_____ computer in your bedroom?

B: Yes, there is.

◯/⑤

Communication

5 Put the sentences in the dialogue in the correct order.

a ◯ It's in the living room. Let me show you.

b ◯ No, thank you. Where's your new games console?

c ◯ Oh wow! Cool!

d ◯0◯ Hi! Please come in.

e ◯ Thanks.

f ◯ Would you like a drink?

◯/⑤

Vocabulary	◯/⑩
Grammar	◯/⑩
Communication	◯/⑤
Your total score	▭ / 25

Extra Online Practice

Unit 3, Language Revision

Word blog: In the house

1 My photos Label the rooms.

1 _____ 2 _____ 3 _____

2 My chat room Complete the conversation.

What's your favourite place?

My bedroom. I love it! I've got lots
of ¹ _____  on my ² _____ .
And there's a small ³ _____ too.

Cool! Are there any posters on the
⁴ _____ ?

Yes, there are. There are five!

Are you in your room now?

No, I'm not. I'm in on the ⁵ _____
in front of the ⁶ _____ .

Ha! Me too!

3 Get more Match 1–6 to A–F. Which is your favourite?

A
B
C

D
E
F

1 ☐ apple   3 ☐ cupcake   5 ☐ ice cream
2 ☐ ketchup   4 ☐ milk   6 ☐ orange juice

Get more words

Yummy!

Yuck!

Fun Spot

What's wrong? In your notebook, write five sentences. Use the ideas in the box.

bath   bed   cat   chairs   desk   fridge   plants   TV   wardrobe

There aren't any chairs in the kitchen.

33

About me

4.1 Vocabulary

1 Complete words 1–6 describing the face.

1 e*ar*_____
2 h_____
3 e_____
4 n_____
5 t_____
6 m_____

2 Match 1–4 to A–D.

1 eyes [B]
2 teeth [ ]
3 ears [ ]
4 nose [ ]

(A)

(B)

(C)

(D)

LOOK! Maria's hair is brown

3 Look at the pictures. Circle the correct answers.

 1 (short)/ long
blond / red

 2 straight / spiky
red / black

 3 curly / wavy
black / blond

 4 short / long
black / blond

4 Look and complete the sentences.

1 His hair is s *h o r t*
and s_ _ _ _.

2 Her hair is l_ _ _ an
s_ _ _ _ _ _ _.

3 His hair is c_ _ _ _
and b_ _ _ _.

4 Her hair is w_ _ _
and b_ _ _ _.

LOOK!
long/short curly/straight blond/brown/red hair
big/small blue/brown eyes

5 Put the words in the correct order.

1 blond straight short hair
short straight blond hair

2 big eyes blue

_____

3 brown long hair curly

_____

4 red short hair wavy

_____

5 small eyes brown

_____

6 Do these words describe eyes or hair? Write E (eyes) or H (hair).

1 wavy [H]
2 big [ ]
3 blond [ ]
4 straight [ ]
5 short [ ]
6 small [ ]

I remem
that

have got affirmative and negative

+	I/You've (have) got long legs.
	He/She/It's (has) got long legs.
	We/You/They've (have) got long legs.
–	I/You haven't (have not) got long legs.
	He/She/It hasn't (has not) got long legs.
	We/You/They haven't (have not) got long legs.

Complete the sentences with 've got, 's got, haven't got or hasn't got.

1 I've got blue eyes.
  I _haven't got_ green eyes.

2 She _____ long hair.
  She hasn't got short hair.

3 Ben and Tommy have got curly hair.
  They _____ straight hair.

4 You _____ small feet.
  You haven't got big feet.

5 Matt's got dark hair.
  He _____ blond hair.

6 We _____ brown eyes.
  We haven't got black eyes.

Write affirmative (✔) and negative (✘) sentences.

1 Alex / new mobile phone ✔
  Alex has got a new mobile phone.

2 he / a new skateboard ✘
  _____

3 Jen / a new coat ✘
  _____

4 she / a new skirt ✔
  _____

5 Alex and Jen / a cat ✘
  _____

6 they / a games console ✔
  _____

3 **Vocabulary** Match 1–5 to parts of the body. Use the words in the box.

arm   feet   fingers   hands   head
neck   toes

1 _head_   2 _____   3 _____

4 _____ and _____   5 _____ and _____

L☺OK! finger – fingers   foot – feet
          leg – legs   tooth – teeth

4 **Complete the texts with plural nouns. Then match the texts to the photos.**

1 ☐

I've got four short ¹_legs_ (leg).
My ²_____ (foot) are small.
I've got two ³_____ (eye),
a big head and very big
⁴_____ (tooth)!

A
a snake

2 ☐

I've got a long body.
I haven't got any ⁵_____ (leg)
or ⁶_____ (foot). I've got two
big ⁷_____ (eye). I haven't got
any ⁸_____ (ear).

B
a crocodile

✱ 5 **Complete the text with affirmative (✔) and negative (✘) forms of the verb have got.**

Hi! My name is Ben. I'm eleven. I ¹'_ve got_ (✔)
two sisters. I ²_____ (✘) any brothers.
We ³_____ (✔) two pets – a rabbit and a cat.
The cat's name is Softy but the rabbit ⁴_____
(✘) a name.

My school is big. We ⁵_____ (✔) lots of teachers.
I'm in class 5. My best friend's name is Zack.
He ⁶_____ (✔) curly brown hair and big ears!

Extra Online Practice

Unit 4, Video and Grammar

have got questions and short answers

?	Short answers
Have I got a friend?	Yes, I have. / No, I haven't.
Have you got a friend?	Yes, you have. / No, you haven't.
Has he/she/it got a friend?	Yes, he/she/it has. / No, he/she/it hasn't.
Have we/you/they got a friend?	Yes, we/you/they have. / No, we/you/they haven't.
What have you got?	I've got super powers!

1 Circle the correct answer.

1 (Have)/ Has X1 and X2 got big heads?
2 *Have / Has* I got super powers?
3 *Have / Has* Dug got a good friend?
4 *Have / Has* you got super ears?

2 Match answers a–d to the questions in Exercise 1.

a ☐ No, I haven't.   c ☐ Yes, he has.
b ☐ No, you haven't.   d ☐ 1 Yes, they have.

3 Order the words to make questions.

1 super powers we got Have ?
   Have we got super powers?
2 got your super powers Have classmates ?
   _____
3 brothers best friend Has your got any ?
   _____
4 you a sister got Have ?
   _____
5 got Have your a computer parents ?
   _____

4 Write short answers for the questions in Exercise 3.

1 *Yes, you have.*   4 _____
2 _____   5 _____
3 _____

LOOK!

it	→	its	The robot's got its battery.
we	→	our	Superdug is our favourite hero!
you	→	your	They are your robots.
they	→	their	Wonder Will is their friend.

5 Look and complete with *Its, Our, Their* or *Your*.

1 My brothers are young. _____ bikes aren't fast.

2 This cat is sma____ _____ legs a__ short.

3 _____ picture is very good.

4 _____ new car is big!

✱6 Complete the dialogues with the words in the box.

| any got Has Have haven't |
| its ~~my~~ Their 've |

A: This is ¹*my* new dog.
B: ²_____ it ³_____ a name?
A: Yes, ⁴_____ name is Tinker.

A: ⁵_____ you got ⁶_____ sisters?
B: Yes, I ⁷_____ got two sisters. ⁸_____ names are Lea and Anika. But I ⁹_____ got any brothers.

🔊 **10 Apologising**

A: I'm so sorry.
  Sorry about that!
  Sorry, my mistake.
  Are you OK?

B: It's OK.
  That's all right.
  No problem.
  I'm fine.

1 Put the sentences in the dialogues in the correct order.

1 a ⬜ Are you sure?
  b ⬜ It's OK.
  c 〔1〕 Oh no! I'm so sorry!
  d ⬜ Yes, I'm fine.

2 a ⬜ Oh, my mistake. Here you are.
  b ⬜ Thanks.
  c ⬜ Hey! That's my book!
  d ⬜ Sorry about that!

3 a ⬜ That's alright. I'm fine.
  b ⬜ Yes, no problem.
  c ⬜ Oops! Sorry!
  d ⬜ Are you sure?

2 Read the dialogues. Circle the correct answer.

1 **A:** I'm sorry.
  B: _____
    ⓐ That's all right.
    b I'm fine.

2 **A:** Sorry about that!
  B: _____
    a No problem.
    b Are you sure?

3 **A:** Are you OK?
  B: _____
    a No problem.
    b Yes, I'm fine.

4 **A:** I'm fine.
  B: _____
    a Are you sure?
    b That's all right.

5 **A:** Where's my book?
  B: _____
    a Sorry, my mistake.
    b Sorry, I've got it.

3 Complete the dialogues with one word in each gap.

1 **A:** I can't find my book!
  B: I've got it! ¹*Sorry* about that.
  A: ² _____ all right.

2 **A:** Oops! I'm so ³ _____ !
  B: It's OK.
  A: Are you ⁴ _____ ?
  B: Yes, I'm ⁵ _____ .

3 **A:** These aren't my keys.
  B: Sorry, my ⁶ _____ . Here you are.
  A: No ⁷ _____ .

4 Look at the picture. Complete the dialogue.

Matt: *Jason, that's my bag!*
Jason: _____
Matt: _____

Extra Online Practice

Unit 4, Video and Communication

Hi. My name's Tim. I'm eleven and I'm from London. I've got two brothers, three sisters and … ten cousins!

My favourite hobby is reading and I've got a lot of books on my desk. I've got a bike and a skateboard, but I'm not very sporty. My best friend is good at football. His name is Max and he's very nice.

Max is my neighbour too. Our favourite place is his garden. We've got a little house in a tree!

Max has got a sister. Her name is Lucy and she's very clever. Max and I are not very good at Maths, but she is very helpful! I like Lucy!

1 Read the text. What is it about? Tick (✔) the correct pictures.

1 ☐ 2 ☐
3 ☐ 4 ☐
5 ☐ 6 ☐

2 Read the text again. Circle T (true) or F (false).

1 Tim's got a big family. (T) / F
2 There are two boys in his family. T / F
3 Max is sporty. T / F
4 Max has got a garden. T / F
5 Lucy is Tim's sister. T / F

3 **Vocabulary** Complete the sentences with the words in the box.

clever   friendly   funny   helpful   ~~sporty~~

Look at my friends and family. They are all very nice.

This is my dad. He's ¹*sporty* and ²_____ .

This is Damian. He's my cousin. He's very ³_____ .

This is my friend, Paul. He's ⁴_____ .

Silvia is my sister. She is ⁵_____ .

🔊 11 Listen and put the photos in the correct order. Write 1–3.

a panda ☐   a dolphin ☐   an ostrich ☐

🔊 11 Listen again. Tick (✔) for *yes* and put a cross (✗) for *no*.

	dolphins	pandas	ostriches
friendly	✔		
funny			
clever			

Paragraphs

A paragraph is a part of a text. It's about one main idea. Remember to divide your text into paragraphs!

Read the text. Divide it into two paragraphs.

Elephants are very big! They've got big grey bodies, big ears and very long trunks. Elephants aren't very friendly but sometimes they are helpful. They're clever, too.

trunk

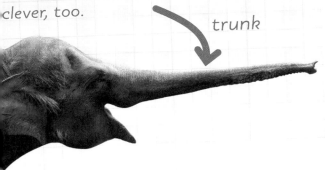

Look at Exercise 3 again. Circle the correct answer.

Paragraph 1 / Paragraph 2 is about elephants' personalities.

5 Write two paragraphs about giraffes. Use the words in the box and your own ideas.

Giraffes
Paragraph 1
tall
long necks   long legs
orange   brown
Paragraph 2
clever (✔)
friendly (✔)

_____Giraffes_____
_____
_____
_____
_____
_____
_____
_____
_____
_____
_____
_____
_____
_____

Vocabulary

1 Match the words to the categories.

> big ~~blond~~ helpful legs nose wavy

Hair: ⁰ _blond_ , ¹ _____
Eyes: ² _____
Face: ³ _____
Body: ⁴ _____
Personality: ⁵ _____

☐/⑤

2 Look at the pictures. Complete the expressions with the words in the box.

> clever curly friendly ~~funny~~
> long straight

0 very _funny_ hair   **1** a very _____ neck

2 long _____ hair   **3** _____ red hair

4 nice and _____   **5** very _____

☐/⑤

Grammar

3 Complete with *have, haven't, has, hasn't* or *got*.

1 A: Mark ⁰ _has_ got brown eyes. ¹ _____ he got brown hair too?
   B: No. His hair is black. His parents and all his brothers have ² _____ black hair.
2 A: ³ _____ you got a new bike?
   B: No, I ⁴ _____ . It's my old bike.
3 Ann ⁵ _____ got any sisters, but she's got one broth⸱

☐/⑤

4 Complete the sentences with *its, your, our* or *their*.

0 Hello. What are _your_ names, please?
1 I have two cousins. _____ names are Clare and Joe
2 Hello, class 2. I'm _____ new teacher.
3 They've got a cat. _____ name is Alfie.
4 We're best friends. _____ names are Katie and Dee
5 My dog is big and _____ ears are long.

☐/⑤

Communication

5 Complete the dialogues with the words in the box.

> all right I'm fine mistake problem
> ~~so sorry~~ you OK

A: Hello, Danny.
B: My name isn't Danny. It's Tom.
A: Oh, I'm ⁰ _so sorry_ !
B: No ¹ _____ !

A: Hey! You've got my bag!
B: Ooops. My ² _____ ! Sorry.
A: That's ³ _____ .

A: Ouch! Your bag is on my foot!
B: Sorry! Are ⁴ _____ ?
A: Yes, ⁵ _____ .

☐/⑤

Vocabulary ☐/⑩
Grammar ☐/⑩
Communication ☐/⑤
Your total score ☐ / 25

Extra Online Practice

Unit 4, Language Revision

Word blog: About me

1 My quiz Complete the sentences and write A or B.

A   B

1 It's got a big _____ ⬜
2 Its _____ is small. ⬜
3 It hasn't got big _____ . ⬜
4 Its _____ are long. ⬜
5 It hasn't got any _____ . ⬜

2 My blog Complete the text with the words from the box.

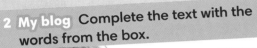

blue   blond   funny   good   sporty   subject

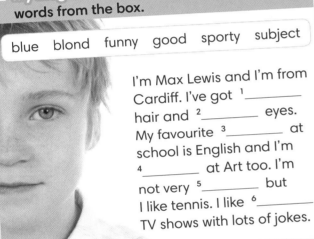

I'm Max Lewis and I'm from Cardiff. I've got ¹_____ hair and ²_____ eyes. My favourite ³_____ at school is English and I'm ⁴_____ at Art too. I'm not very ⁵_____ but I like tennis. I like ⁶_____ TV shows with lots of jokes.

3 Get more Circle the correct answer.

1
A: Where is my *car key / house key*?
B: It's on the table.

2
A: How many *powers / batteries* have you got?
B: I've got two.

3
A: Is English your favourite subject?
B: Yes! And I've got *good marks / bad marks*!

Get more words

He's **good at** sports.

Find five body words and five personality words. In your notebook, put them into two groups.

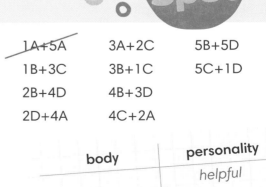

Fun Spot

	A	B	C	D
1	~~HEL~~	CLE	E	NDLY
2	OT	HA	GER	NI
3	FIN	TO	VER	NNY
4	CE	FU	FO	ND
5	~~PFUL~~	MO	FRIE	UTH

~~1A+5A~~   3A+2C   5B+5D
1B+3C   3B+1C   5C+1D
2B+4D   4B+3D
2D+4A   4C+2A

body	personality
	helpful

Patty's blog

My new band!

I'm in a band with Jake and Mick from my class. They're in our practice room in the photo – my garage!

Jake and Mick are both really nice. Jake's twelve. He's got very short, dark hair and big brown eyes. He's tall. He's good at the guitar because he's got big hands and long fingers. Mick's eleven. He's got blond wavy hair and small brown eyes. He's short. He's good at the guitar too.

I've got a guitar but I'm the singer in our band. It's Saturday today and I've got a singing lesson.

My teacher's very funny.
Bye!

Reading and Writing

1 Read the text. Circle T (true) or F (false).

0	There are four children in the band.	T /F
1	Jake is short.	T / F
2	Jake hasn't got blond hair.	T / F
3	Mick's got wavy hair and big brown eyes.	T / F
4	Mick is good at the guitar.	T / F
5	Patty hasn't got a guitar.	T / F

☐/⑤

2 Complete the text with the words in the box. There is one extra word.

> are   behind   ~~house~~   got   kitchen   old
> sister   small   upstairs

We've got a new **0**_house_! There **1**_____ two bedrooms, one for me and my **2**_____ and one for my parents. The living room, **3**_____ and bathroom are downstairs. There is a **4**_____ garden and there's a garage too. We've **5**_____ a lot of things. Some things are in the garage! There's an **6**_____ bed next to one wall. My bike is **7**_____ mum's car and dad's car is outside in front of the garage! My new house is cool.

3 Write five sentences about Danny. Use the information in the table.

0 Name	Danny
1 Nationality	🇺🇸
2 Hair	
3 Eyes	
4 Personality	friendly, funny
5 Family	two sisters

0 _His name's Danny._

1 _____

_____

2 _____

_____

3 _____

_____

4 _____

_____

5 _____

_____

☐/⑦   ☐/⑧

Listening

4 🔊 12 **Listen and tick (✔) the correct answer.**

0 What has Anne got?

A ☐

B ☐

C ☑

1 Where's Charlie's computer?

A ☐

B ☐

C ☐

2 Who is in the garden?

A ☐

B ☐

C ☐

3 Who is Charlie's cousin?

A ☐

B ☐

C ☐

4 What's under the table?

A ☐

B ☐

C ☐

☐/4

Communication

5 The Smith family are at granny and grandad's new house. Match pictures 0–4 to sentences a–g. There are two extra sentences.

a Let me show you.

b There aren't any plants.

c Would you like an ice cream?

d I'm fine.

e I'm so sorry!

f Please come in.

g Look! There's a big garden!

☐/4

Reading and Writing ☐ /17
Listening ☐ /4
Communication ☐ /4
Your total score ☐ / 25

Things I can do

5.1 Vocabulary

1 Look at the picture. Match a–h to 1–8.

1	[f] jump	5	[ ] ride
2	[ ] draw	6	[ ] run
3	[ ] fly	7	[ ] skateboard
4	[ ] dive	8	[ ] swim

2 Cross out two letters to find action verbs.

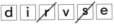

d i ~~r~~ v ~~s~~ e   a e c t m   i s i r n g

1 _dive_   2 _____   3 _____

c o r o a k   w o r i t d e

4 _____   5 _____

3 Complete the sentences with the words in the box.

| Climb Fly ~~Fix~~ Read Ride Write |

1 _Fix_ it, please.   2 _____ the kite.

3 _____ the stairs.   4 _____ the book

5 _____ your name, please.   6 _____ your bike

I rememb that!

4 Complete the expressions with action verbs.

1 _read_ a

2 _____ a wardrobe with a

3 _____ with a

4 _____ in new

5 _____ with

can affirmative and negative

+	I/You/He/She/It/We/They **can** jump.
–	I/You/He/She/It/We/They **can't** jump.

1 Circle the correct answer.

1 The girl (can)/ can't read.
2 The man *can / can't* cook.
3 The cat *can / can't* write.

4 She *can / can't* run.
5 He *can / can't* fix bikes.
6 The bird *can / can't* fly.

Put the words in the correct order to make sentences.

1 sing well can I .
   I can sing well.
2 fast run Sam can't .
   _____
3 can football Grandad play .
   _____
4 skateboard can't Mum .
   _____
5 very Sally can't well cook .
   _____

3 Write sentences with *can* or *can't*.

1 Lian / draw animals ✔
   Lian *can draw animals* _____ .
2 Lucas / sing well ✗
   Lucas _____ .
3 Alex / fix computers ✔
   Alex _____ .
4 Granny / play the guitar ✗
   Granny _____ .
5 Jen / make cupcakes ✔
   Jen _____ .

4 Are sentences 1–6 true? Answer *yes* (✔) or *no* (✗). Correct the false sentences.

1 Cats can't climb trees. ☒ *Cats can climb trees.*
2 Rabbits can jump. ☐ _____
3 I can fly. ☐ _____
4 Dogs can read. ☐ _____
5 My friend can't cook. ☐ _____
6 I can't read Chinese. ☐ _____

> **LOOK!** play football
> play **the** piano

5 Vocabulary Complete with *play*, *make* or *ride*. What about you? Tick (✔) for *yes*.

1 *play* basketball ☐
2 _____ a poster ☐
3 _____ a horse ☐
4 _____ a bike ☐
5 _____ the piano ☐
6 _____ cupcakes ☐

✱ 6 Complete with *can*, *can't* and the words in the box to make sentences that are true for you.

fix make play run ride ~~speak~~

1 I *can speak* English.
2 I _____ the guitar.
3 I _____ cakes.
4 I _____ computers.
5 I _____ a horse.
6 I _____ fast.

> **Extra Online Practice**
>
> Unit 5, Video and Grammar

can questions and short answers

?	Short answers
Can I swim?	Yes, I can. / No, I can't.
Can you swim?	Yes, you can. / No, you can't.
Can he/she/it swim?	Yes, he/she/it can. / No, he/she/it can't.
Can we/you/they swim?	Yes, we/you/they can. / No, we/you/they can't.
What can we do?	We can help.

1 Read the sentences and write questions.

1 They can swim. _Can they swim?_

2 I can draw. _____

3 Tom can run fast. _____

4 May can sing well. _____

5 We can help. _____

6 The cat can climb. _____

2 Look at the picture. Answer the questions with the short answers in the box.

| Yes, he can.   No, he can't.   No, she can't. |
| No, it can't.   ~~Yes, they can.~~   No, they can't. |

1 Can Kit and Dug see the boat? _Yes, they can._

2 Can the boy and girl swim? _____

3 Can their mum swim? _____

4 Can Dug swim? _____

5 Can the small dog help? _____

6 Can Dug help? _____

3 Write questions.

1 you / fix a bike?
  Can you fix a bike?

2 you / play volleyball?
  _____

3 your mum / speak English?
  _____

4 your classmates / speak Spanish?
  _____

5 you / ride a horse?
  _____

6 your best friend / play the piano?
  _____

4 Answer the questions in Exercise 3 so that they are true for you.

1 _____

2 _____

3 _____

4 _____

5 _____

6 _____

✱5 Complete the dialogues with the correct form of the verb can and the verbs in the box.

| dance   help   play   see |

1 A: ¹ _Can_ you ² _____ those red apples?
   B: Yes, I ³ _____ .
   A: ⁴ _____ you ⁵ _____ me, please? I'm too sho
   B: No problem.

2 A: ⁶ _____ they ⁷ _____ ?
   B: Yes, they ⁸ _____ .
   A: ⁹ _____ the girl ¹⁰ _____ the piano too?
   B: No, she ¹¹ _____ .

13 Suggestions

A: Let's *do something fun*!
Let's *go ice skating*!
We can *go to the park*!

B: 🙂 I agree!
Let's do that!
Great idea!

😐 I'm not sure.

🙁 It's not a good idea.

Match 1–6 to a–f.

1 [e] Let's play
2 [ ] We can watch
3 [ ] Let's have a party
4 [ ] Let's ride
5 [ ] We can go to
6 [ ] Let's make

a the park.
b for your birthday.
c chocolate cupcakes.
d our bikes.
e football after school.
f my new DVD.

Complete the expressions and draw a face.

1 Let's do <u>t h a t</u>! 🙂

2 It's not a _ _ _ _ idea. 😐

3 Great _ _ _ _! 😐

4 I'm not _ _ _ _. 😐

5 I _ _ _ _ _. 😐

Put the sentences in the dialogue in the correct order.

a [ ] We haven't got a ball.
b [ ] No, not the garden again. We can go to the park.
c [ ] Why not?
d [1] Hi! Let's play in the garden.
e [ ] I'm not sure about football.
f [ ] Yes, the park's a great idea. We can play football.

4 Circle the correct answer.

1 A: Let's watch TV.
　B: Yes, I _____ .
　　(a) agree　　　　b 'm sure

2 A: Let's _____ to the park.
　B: OK.
　　a go　　　　　b going

3 A: We can play a computer game.
　B: _____
　　a Great idea!　b Yes, I can.

4 A: Let's have ice cream.
　B: _____
　　a No, thank you.　b It's not a good idea.

5 A: We _____ make sandwiches.
　B: Let's do that!
　　a can　　　　　b can't

5 Write the suggestions and replies.

1
A: play a game
B: 🙂
A: *We can play a game!*
B: _____

2
A: watch that
B: 😐
A: _____
B: _____

3
A: go there
B: 🙁
A: _____
B: _____

Extra Online Practice

Unit 5, Video and Communication

Twelve-year-old Jasmine and her best friend are always together. Her best friend isn't a girl or a boy. He's a very special dog, called Sweep.

Jasmine is an ordinary girl but she's got a problem – she can't hear. Think about it. She can't hear people, she can't hear music or the TV. She can't even hear cars in the street. It is sometimes very dangerous for her. But Jasmine is OK, because she's got Sweep, and Sweep is her ears! Sweep is a special 'hearing dog'. He can help Jasmine a lot. These days Jasmine can meet all her friends and hang out with them after school. Her parents can relax because Sweep is with her and she's safe.

1 Look at the pictures and complete the sentences.

1 You can see people with your **e _ _s.**

2 You can hear music with your **e_ _s.**

3 You can smell flowers with your **n_ _ e.**

2 Complete the text with the words in the box.

friends hands hear ~~Look~~

¹ _Look_ at these women. They can't ² _____ , but they can make words with their ³ _____ . It's a special sign language. They can use it to speak to their ⁴ _____ and family.

3 Read the text and choose the best title. Circle the correct answer.

a A dog helps a girl called Jasmine.
b A girl called Jasmine helps her pet dog.
c A dog called Sweep has got a problem.

4 Read the text again. Circle the correct answer.

1 Sweep is *a boy* / (*a dog*).
2 *Jasmine* / *Sweep* can't hear.
3 Jasmine has got *one friend* / *lots of friends*.
4 Jasmine *can* / *can't* visit people.
5 Jasmine's mum and dad *are* / *aren't* always with her.

5 Read the text again. Match 1–6 to a–f.

1 [b] Jasmine has
2 [ ] Sweep is Jasmine's
3 [ ] Sweep can
4 [ ] Jasmine's best friend
5 [ ] Jasmine's parents
6 [ ] Jasmine is safe

a help Jasmine.   d with Sweep.
b got a problem.   e ears.
c are happy.   f is a dog.

1 What's this? Put the letters in the correct order.

e	d	a	t	y	r	e	b	d
1	2	3	4	5	6	7	8	9

4	1	9	2	5

8	7	3	6

2 🔊 **14** Listen and circle the correct answer.

At this club you can *make a new teddy bear /
fix an old teddy bear*.

🔊 **14** Listen again. Which is the correct teddy bear?
Tick (✔).

A ☐   B ☐   C ☐

🔊 **14** Listen again. Circle the correct answer.

1 What is the girl's name?
Her name is *Sarah / Erin*.

2 Is the teddy bear Tommy's or his sister's?
It's *Tommy's / his sister's*.

3 Can Sarah fix it?
Yes, she can. / No, she can't.

4 What colour are the new eyes?
They're black. / They're blue.

and, but

You **can** make robots *and* you **can** play
computer games.
You **can** write emails *but* you **can't** write
computer programs.

5 Complete the blog post with *and* or *but*.

Come to our
new **Fix It Club!**
It's fun ¹ _and_
it's free! We can fix
clothes ² _____ bikes.
We can fix computers ³ _____
we can't fix cars. Sorry! You can watch us
⁴ _____ learn to fix things too. We are
at the Youth Club every Saturday morning,
⁵ _____ not in the afternoon.
Come and visit us soon!

6 Write a blog post about the Basketball Club.
Use these notes.

BASKETBALL CLUB

learn to play • watch great games •

make friends • have fun • in the School Hall •

every Sunday • not in school holidays

Come to our new BASKETBALL CLUB

_____
_____
_____
_____
_____
_____
_____
_____
_____
_____
_____

Vocabulary

1 What can they do? Write the action verbs.

0 ___fly___

1 _____

2 _____

3 _____

4 _____

5 _____

☐/⑤

2 Circle the correct word.

0 (draw) / read a picture
1 play / ride the guitar
2 make / play a cupcake
3 sing / read a book
4 ride / dive a bike
5 act / play computer games

☐/⑤

Grammar

3 Look at the table. Complete the sentences with *can*, *can't*, *and* or *but*.

	swim	run fast	fix a bike
Anna	✔	✔	✘
Tom	✘	✔	✔
Sam and Joe	✔	✔	✘

Anna can swim ⁰ _and_ she ⁰⁰ _can_ run fast.
Tom ¹_____ run fast ²_____ he can fix a bike.
Sam and Joe can swim fast ³_____ they ⁴_____
fix a bike. Tom and Anna ⁵_____ run fast.

☐/⑤

4 Look at the picture. Write questions. Answer *yes* (✔) or *no* (✘). Use short answers.

1 she / play the piano
   A: ⁰*Can she play the piano* ?
   B: ✔ ¹_____
2 the dogs / sing
   A: ²_____
   B: ✘ ³_____
3 the boy / ride his bike
   A: ⁴_____
   B: ✔ ⁵_____

☐/⑤

Communication

5 Complete the dialogue with one word in each gap.

Amy: ⁰ _Let's_ do something.
Jack: OK. We ¹_____ make a chocolate cake!
Amy: I'm not ²_____ . I ³_____ cook very well.
Jack: No ⁴_____ . I can teach you.
Amy: OK, cool. ⁵_____ idea!

☐/⑤

Vocabulary	☐/⑩
Grammar	☐/⑩
Communication	☐/⑤
Your total score	/ 25

Extra Online Practice

Unit 5, Language Revision

Word blog: What can you do?

1 My quiz Label the pictures. What can you do? Tick (✔).

 1 ☐ p_ _ _ f_ _ _ _ _ _ _

 2 ☐ r_ _

 3 ☐ s_ _ _

 4 ☐ r_ _ _ a h_ _ _ _

 5 ☐ j_ _ _

2 My chat room Complete the conversation with one word in each gap.

Hi! Let's ¹_____ our bikes to the park.

Sorry, I can't. There's something ²_____ with my bike.

OK. ³_____ you swim?

Yes. Why?

We can go to the swimming ⁴_____ .

Great ⁵_____ . Then we can ⁶_____ a computer game at my house.

3 Get more Complete the text with the words in the box.

| words | letters | alphabet |

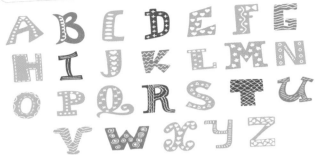

This is the English ¹_____ . There are 26 ²_____ in English. You use them to make ³_____ .

Get more words

She's talented. She can run very fast.

What can you see in the room? Complete the sentences with *can* and *can't*.

1 He _____ play the guitar.
2 He _____ skateboard.
3 He _____ play the piano.
4 He _____ fix things.
5 He _____ fly.
6 He _____ sing.
7 He _____ draw.
8 He _____ cook.

1 What can you do in this room? Tick (✔) for *yes* and put a cross (✗) for *no*.

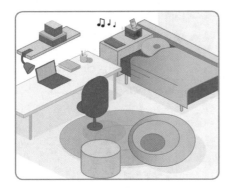

1
- ✔ tidy my room
- ☐ have a shower
- ☐ listen to music
- ☐ do my homework
- ☐ hang out with my friends

2
- ☐ have lessons
- ☐ have lunch
- ☐ watch TV
- ☐ get up
- ☐ have breakfast

LOOK! have breakfast/lunch/dinner
have **a** shower
have lesson**s**

2 Find and circle eight words. Then complete the expressions.

F	D	R	R	E	W	O	R	Y	T	C	S
R	I	H	O	M	E	W	O	R	K	A	H
I	N	O	L	U	Y	F	O	P	P	O	O
E	N	T	V	S	G	E	M	X	I	W	W
N	E	E	Q	I	E	C	K	D	S	S	E
D	R	R	S	C	H	O	O	L	O	M	R

1 do my *homework*
2 tidy my _____
3 have _____
4 have a _____
5 listen to _____
6 go to _____
7 watch _____
8 hang out with my _____

3 Complete the sentences with the words in the box.

do   get up   go   go   ~~have~~   have

1 I ___*have*___ lessons.
2 I _____ in the morning.
3 I _____ my homework.
4 I _____ to bed.
5 I _____ to school.
6 I _____ breakfast.

4 Write the sentences in Exercise 3 in the order you do them on a typical day.

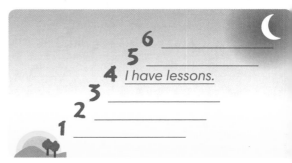

6 _____
5 _____
4 *I have lessons.*
3 _____
2 _____
1 _____

I remember that!

5 Look and cross out the wrong answer.

in the bathroom
listen to music /
have a shower /
~~have lessons~~

in the living room
get up / watch TV /
hang out with
friends

in the kitchen
tidy my room /
listen to music /
have breakfast

in the bedroom
do homework /
have a shower /
go to bed

Present Simple affirmative

✚	I/You	listen to music.
	He/She/It	listens to music.
	We/You/They	listen to music.

Circle the correct answer.

1 Jen *watch* / *watches* TV after dinner.
2 Alex *do* / *does* his homework in his room.
3 Lucas and Alex *play* / *plays* football in the park.
4 Jen and Alex *get up* / *gets up* late.
5 Lucas's mum *listen* / *listens* to music in the kitchen.
6 Lucas *go* / *goes* to school with Jen and Alex.

LOOK!

get → gets   watch → watches   tidy → tidies
make → makes   go → goes   have → has

Complete the table.

I/you/we/they	he/she/it
play	¹*plays*
² _____	does
draw	³ _____
⁴ _____	drinks
⁵ _____	looks
wash	⁶ _____
⁷ _____	carries

Write sentences about Sam.

1 I have breakfast at 7 o'clock.

Sam has breakfast at 7 o'clock.

2 I go to school with my sister.

_____

3 I do my homework before dinner.

_____

4 I watch TV after dinner.

_____

5 I play football with my friends.

_____

4 Complete the sentences. Put the verbs in the correct form.

1 My brother and I __*like*__ (like) orange juice but my sister _____ (drink) milk.
2 Mum and dad _____ (watch) TV and my sister and I _____ (play) computer games after dinner.
3 Rob _____ (tidy) his room and he _____ (help) in the kitchen too.
4 Sue _____ (have) sandwiches for lunch. She _____ (eat) them in the classroom.
5 I _____ (hang out) with my friends after school. Then I _____ (have) dinner.
6 Harry _____ (do) his homework and then he _____ (watch) TV.

✱ **5 Complete the table. Write sentences that are true for you.**

	Laura	Me
1 has lunch		_____
2 do my homework		_____
3 play		_____
4 like		_____

1 Laura __*has lunch at school*__.
I _____ .
2 Laura _____ her _____ .
I _____ my _____ .
3 Laura _____ .
_____ .
4 Laura _____ .
_____ .

Extra Online Practice
Unit 6, Video and Grammar

Adverbs of frequency

■■■■	We always hang out with our friends.
■■■□	He usually goes to the gym.
■■□□	I often visit my grandma.
■□□□	She sometimes has dinner with us.
□□□□	They never get up late.

1 Complete the sentences with adverbs of frequency.

1 Jack ■□□□ *sometimes* cycles to school.
2 Emma ■■■■ _____ has breakfast at home.
3 Pete ■■■□ _____ does his homework in his bedroom.
4 I ■□□□ _____ play in the park.
5 We □□□□ _____ watch TV in the morning.
6 My parents ■□□□ _____ go out with their friends.

Adverb + verb	Adverb + *to be*
I always have breakfast.	I am always happy.
They never get up late.	They are never late.

2 Rewrite the sentences. Use the word in brackets.

1 I'm busy on Saturdays. (often)
   I'm often busy on Saturdays.
2 Kit helps me at home. (often)
   _____
3 Uncle Roberto visits me. (sometimes)
   _____
4 I cook dinner. (never)
   _____
   _____
5 Kit is happy. (always)
   _____
   _____
6 Kit and I have fun. (usually)
   _____
   _____

3 Vocabulary Complete the days of week. Then put them in the correct orde

```
We _ _ esday
_ ue _ day
1  M o n day
Sat _ _ day
_ u _ day
Th _ r _ day
_ r _ day
```

4 Look at the information about Tom and write sentences.

1 be late for school?
   never

2 get up late?
   usually (on Sund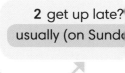

5 play computer games?
   sometimes

4 play football?
   often (on Saturday)

3 be happ
   usually

1 Tom *is never late for school* .
2 He _____ .
3 He _____ .
4 He _____ .
5 He _____ .

✱5 Look at Exercise 4 again. Write sentence that are true for you.

1 I _____ late for school.
2 _____
3 _____
4 _____
5 _____

 **15 Telling the time**

A: What time is it?

B: It's 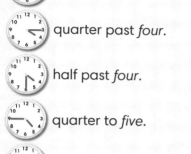 *four* o'clock.

A: What time is the *film/match*?

B: It's at *ten* (minutes) past *four*.

quarter past *four*.

half past *four*.

quarter to *five*.

ten (minutes) to *five*.

Match clocks a–h to expressions 1–8.

 a

 b

 c

 d

 e

 f

 g

 h

1 [b] six o'clock
2 ☐ quarter to five
3 ☐ half past two
4 ☐ five to one
5 ☐ quarter past one
6 ☐ five past five
7 ☐ twenty to nine
8 ☐ ten past nine

2 Complete the sequences.

1 twelve o'clock – five past twelve – ¹*ten past twelve* – quarter past twelve – ² _____ – twenty-five past twelve – ³ _____

2 half past two – ⁴ _____ – twenty to three – quarter to three – ⁵ _____ – ⁶ _____ – three o'clock

3 Look at the TV schedule. Then complete the questions and answers.

06:00	06:35	07:05	07:15	07:50
Pet Time	Super Girl	Happy Days	That's Magic	The Great Big Talent Show

1 A: What time is *Pet Time*?
  B: *It's at six o'clock.*

2 A: What time is *That's Magic*?
  B: _____

3 A: _____ ?
  B: It's at five past seven.

4 A: _____ ?
  B: It's at twenty-five to seven.

5 A: What time is *the Great Big Talent Show*?
  B: _____

6 A: OK. _____ now?
  B: It's five to six. Hurry up!

4 Put the dialogue in the correct order.

a [1] What time is it, Mandy?
b ☐ No, I'm not. I'm late for my music lesson.
c ☐ It's at quarter to six. Bye!
d ☐ It's half past five. Oh no!
e ☐ What's wrong? Are you OK?
f ☐ Oh dear. What time is your music lesson?

5 Complete the sentences for you.

1 I get up at _____ .
2 I have breakfast at _____ .
3 I go to school at _____ .
4 I do my homework at _____ .
5 I go to bed at _____ .

 Extra Online Practice

Unit 6, Video and Communication

Reading

> Hi. I'm Mike. I'm ten and I'm American. I live in New York. My school is very big. I like sport. I'm not very good at Art but I love it. I have lunch in the classroom. I usually have pizza! After school I always hang out with my friends. We sometimes play basketball or we go to the park.

> My name is Dasha and I'm nine. I go to a special school. It's a ballet school! After breakfast we have lessons. My favourite lessons are Maths and English. Then we have lunch. I often have pancakes! After lunch we always dance. I'm always busy.

1 Read the texts. Match photos A–F to Mike or Dasha.

1 Mike [B] [ ] [ ]
2 Dasha [ ] [ ] [ ]

A

B

C

D

E

F

2 Read the texts again. Circle T (true) or F (false).

1 Mike likes Art.   (T)/ F
2 He eats pizza in the classroom.   T / F
3 He never goes to the park after school. T / F
4 Dasha likes Maths.   T / F
5 She has pancakes every day.   T / F
6 She has lessons after lunch.   T / F

3 Read the texts again. Complete the sentences with one or two words in each gap.

1 Mike goes to a _____ school.
2 He plays basketball with _____
3 Dasha _____ after breakfast.
4 Dasha is always _____ .

4 **Vocabulary** Order the letters to make months.

1 ecmeDreb   _December_
2 barrFeuy   _____
3 nJeu   _____
4 oOcbetr   _____
5 priAl   _____
6 utgusA   _____

5 Complete with the words in Exercise 4

January	¹_____	March
²_____	May	³_____
July	⁴_____	September
⁵_____	November	⁶ _Decembe_

1 🔊 **16 Listen to Andy and complete the notes.**

Andy's holidays

Country: ¹ *Italy*

Aunt's nationality: ² _____

Aunt's job: ³ _____

Favourite place: ⁴ _____

Favourite game: ⁵ _____

2 🔊 **16 Listen again. Circle the correct word.**

1 Andy (always)/ usually goes on holiday in August.
2 After breakfast they *usually / often* go to the beach.
3 They *always / often* have a picnic on the beach.
4 They *usually / often* go to bed after lunch.
5 He *always / never* gets up early.

before, after

```
                  lunch
●━━━━━━━━━●━━━━━━━●━━━━━━━▶
tidy my              play computer
room                 games
```

Before lunch I tidy my room.
I tidy my room *before* lunch.

After lunch I play computer games.
I play computer games *after* lunch.

Circle *before* and *after* in Jane's blog post.

```
☰                                    ↻

   A u g u s t

We never go to school in August.
It's a holiday! I get up late. I often play
computer games (before) breakfast. I never
have breakfast in bed. I have it in the
kitchen. After breakfast I often hang out
with friends. Before dinner I sometimes
help my parents. I usually watch TV after
dinner. I often go to bed late.
```

4 Read the blog again. Put the activities in the boxes in the correct order.

> ~~get up~~   hang out with friends
> have breakfast   play computer games

Before lunch

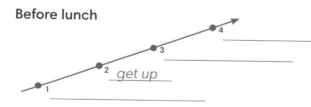

After lunch

> go to bed   have dinner
> help my parents   watch TV

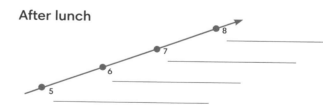

5 Write about your typical holiday day. Use *before* and *after*.

_____
_____
_____
_____
_____
_____
_____
_____

Vocabulary

1 Complete the sentences with one word in each gap.

0 In the morning, I _get_ up at 7 o'clock.

1 We _____ lessons all day.

2 After school, I _____ out with friends.

3 We _____ computer games on Saturdays.

4 Before bed, I _____ TV.

5 At night, I _____ to bed at 9.

☐/⑤

2 Complete the sequences.

0 January | *February* | March

1 July | _____ | September

2 Friday | _____ | Sunday

3 October | _____ | December

4 March | _____ | May

5 Tuesday | _____ | Thursday

☐/⑤

Grammar

3 Complete the sentences. Put the verbs in the correct form.

0 Tom _gets up_ (get up) early.

1 We _____ (go) to a big school.

2 Sally _____ (like) chocolate ice crea[m]

3 Harry _____ (tidy) his room on Sund[ay]

4 They _____ (do) their homework in th[e] living room.

5 I _____ (have) lunch in the park.

☐/[5]

4 Put the words in the correct order.

0 walk They always school to .
They always walk to school.

1 always I busy am .
_____

2 play We tennis often .
_____

3 watches never Mum TV .
_____

4 I room sometimes my tidy .
_____

5 is Jess late usually .
_____

☐/[

Communication

5 Complete the dialogues with one word in each gap.

1 A: What ⁰ _time_ is lunch?
B: It's at half ¹_____ twelve.

2 A: What time ²_____ it?
B: It's ten ³_____ to five.

3 A: What time is the film?
B: It's ⁴_____ six o'⁵_____ .

☐/[

Vocabulary	☐/[10]
Grammar	☐/[10]
Communication	☐/[5]
Your total score	/ 25

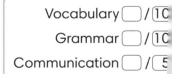

Extra Online Practice

Unit 6, Language Revision

Word blog: My day

1 My photos Look and complete.

1 I get up at _h_ _a_ _l_ _f_ _ _ _ _ six .

2 I have a _ _ _ _ _ _ at seven _ _ _ _ _ _ _ .

3 I have _ _ _ _ _ at _ _ _ _ _ _ _ to one.

4 I _ _ my homework at half past _ _ _ _ .

3 Get more Match 1–4 to a–d to make expressions.

play 1

a Australia
my grandparents

go 2

computer games
b with my pet
the piano

have 3

c dinner
swimming lessons

visit 4

to bed
d to the gym
to the cinema

2 My quiz Read and complete.

the day ¹before Monday	the day after ² _____	the day before Thursday
Sunday	Saturday	³ _____

the month ⁴ _____ May	the month after ⁵ _____	the month after January
April	July	⁶ _____

Get more words

Get ready for school!

Look at the pictures. In your notebook, write what Daisy does on Saturdays.

Fun Spot

- always
- usually
- sometimes
- never

Daisy sometimes tidies her room on Saturdays.

My week

I always get up at half past six. I have breakfast and then I go to school. My school is a special dancing school. We have dancing lessons after school on Mondays, Wednesdays and Fridays. We run, jump and dance! We often make videos. That's very cool. Then I go home and do my homework. I have dinner and speak to my family. I usually go to bed at half past nine.

At the weekend I usually hang out with my best friend, Madalena. We are classmates. We speak about our lessons and watch videos about our favourite dancers.

My name is Justine. I'm eleven and I'm a dancer. I'm sometimes on TV!

Reading and Writing

1 Read the text. What is it about? Circle the correct answer.

   a A girl.
   b A school. ☐/①

2 Read the text again. Circle T (true) or F (false).

0 Justine can dance.   Ⓣ/ F
1 Justine gets up early.   T / F
2 Justine never has breakfast at school.   T / F
3 Her dancing lessons are on Thursdays. T / F
4 The students never make videos in their dancing lessons.   T / F
5 Madalena isn't Justine's sister.   T / F
6 Justine and Madalena make videos at the weekend.   T / F

☐/⑥

3 Complete the text with the words in the box. There are two extra words.

My day

I get up early every day. I have a ⁰ *shower* and then I have breakfast. Mum sometimes makes ¹_____! I usually ride my bike to school. I always do my ²_____ at school after lessons. Then I go home and I tidy my ³_____ . I have dinner with my family and we all watch ⁴_____ . I sometimes hang out with my ⁵_____ after school on Fridays. We listen to music and we speak about our week.

Example

shower

homework

television

pancakes

computer

bike

friends

bedroom

☐/

4 Write five sentences about what Alice usually does on Mondays.

0 get up `07:15`
1 have breakfast `08:00`
2 go to school `08:30`
3 have lessons all day!
4 do my homework `05:00`
5 have dinner at granny's house `06:45`

0 *Alice gets up at quarter past seven.*
1 _____
2 _____
3 _____
4 _____
5 _____

☐/⑤

Listening

 **17** Julie is with her mum's friend, Mrs Williams. Mrs Williams has got some family photos. Listen and match names 0–4 to pictures A–F. There is one extra picture.

0 Rob `D`   2 Barny ☐   4 May ☐
1 Ann ☐   3 Karen ☐

(A)
(B)
(C)
(D)
(E)
(F)

☐/④

Communication

6 Read the sentences and circle the best answer.

0 **Alex:** Can you sing?
  Kim: A I often sing.
        B Yes, you can!
        Ⓒ Yes, I can!

1 **Alex:** Let's go to Music Club after school.
  Kim: A No thanks. It's cool.
        B Me too.
        C Not again!

2 **Alex:** I know! We can go to the cinema!
  Kim: A I'm fine, thank you!
        B Great idea!
        C It's over there!

3 **Alex:** What time is the film?
  Kim: A It's at half past five.
        B It's on Wednesday.
        C It's very funny.

4 **Alex:** Let's ask Michelle to come.
  Kim: A OK, we can phone her.
        B Michelle, here you are.
        C OK, Michelle can help.

☐/④

Reading and Writing ☐/⑰
Listening ☐/④
Communication ☐/④
Your total score ▢ / 25

7 Animals

7.1 Vocabulary

1 Match animals a–h to words 1–8.

 a
 b
 c
 d
 e
 f
 g
 h

1 [d] crocodile   5 [ ] lion
2 [ ] frog   6 [ ] monkey
3 [ ] butterfly   7 [ ] snake
4 [ ] kangaroo   8 [ ] whale

2 Which animal is different? Circle the odd one out. Match it to the correct reason.

1 [c] fish   crocodile   frog   (kangaroo)
2 [ ] spider   butterfly   bird   fly
3 [ ] elephant   fish   monkey   tiger
4 [ ] lion   tiger   giraffe   fly
5 [ ] tiger   whale   snake   fish

a It lives in water.
b It can fly.
c It can't swim.
d It can't fly.
e It's got legs.

3 Circle the correct word.

1 *Frogs /* (*Crocodiles*) have got big teeth.
2 *Whales / Frogs* live in the sea.
3 *Spiders / Snakes* are very long.
4 *Tigers / Birds* can fly.
5 *Frogs / Snakes* can jump.
6 *Spiders / Lions* have got eight legs.

4 Complete the puzzle.

```
1 [ ][ ][ ][ ][G][ ][ ][ ]
     2 [ ][ ][I][ ][ ]
   3 [ ][ ][R][ ][ ]
 4 [ ][ ][ ][A][ ]
       5 [ ][F][ ][ ]
     6 [ ][ ][F][ ][ ][ ]
7 [ ][ ][ ][ ][E][ ]
```

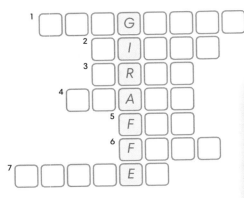

1 It lives in Australia. It can jump.
2 It's a big cat. It's black and yellow.
3 It's small and green. It's got big eyes. It can jump.
4 It's very, very big. It can swim.
5 It's very small. It's black.
6 It hasn't got any legs. It can swim.
7 It's got two arms and two legs. It can climb trees.

> I rememb
> **that!**

5 What can animals do? Write two animals under each verb. Use words in Exercise 2.

swim	run	fly
crocodile	*elephant*	*bird*
_____	_____	_____
_____	_____	_____

Present Simple negative

— I **don't** (do not) get up early.

You **don't** (do not) get up early.

He/She/It **doesn't** (does not) get up early.

We/You/They **don't** (do not) get up early.

1 Put the words in the correct order to make sentences.

1 don't computer parents games play My .
My parents don't play computer games.

2 early I get up on Saturdays don't .
_____

3 Lucy does cats like not .
_____

4 go Josh to school doesn't by bike .
_____

5 Mondays do on hang out not We .
_____

2 Complete the sentences. Put the verbs in the correct form.

1 My pet *doesn't like* (not like) apples.
2 I _____ (not tidy) my room every day.
3 We _____ (not watch) TV before dinner.
4 My little sister _____ (not go) to school.
5 You _____ (not like) pop music.
6 My cousin _____ (not speak) French.

Write affirmative (✔) or negative (✗) sentences.

1 my puppy / ✔ like / TV
My puppy likes TV.

2 cats / ✗ eat / cupcakes
Cats don't eat cupcakes.

3 my friend / ✔ play / in the garden
_____

4 my sister / ✗ tidy / her bedroom
_____

5 Joe and Adam / ✔ hang out / after school
_____

6 we / ✗ go to school / on Sundays
_____

4 Look at the table. Correct the sentences.

	gets up early	play computer games	listen to classical music
Jen	✗	✔	✗
Alex	✗	✔	✔
Mum	✔	✗	✔
Dad	✗	✗	✔

1 Jen, Alex and Dad get up early.
Jen, Alex and Dad don't get up early.

2 Dad gets up early.
_____

3 Jen and Alex don't play computer games.
_____

4 Mum and Dad play computer games.
_____

5 Mum doesn't listen to classical music.
_____

6 Jen listens to classical music.
_____

5 Vocabulary Match animals a–h to sentences 1–8.

1 [a] It's got small ears.   a a hamster
2 [ ] It can fly.   b a tortoise
3 [ ] It lives in water.   c a parrot
4 [ ] It's got long ears.   d a rabbit
5 [ ] It's got a long body.   e a goldfish
6 [ ] It doesn't walk fast!   f an iguana
7 [ ] It likes milk.   g a dog
8 [ ] Its babies are puppies.   h a cat

✱6 Complete the sentences for you.

1 On Wednesdays, I _____ .

2 On Sundays, I don't _____ .

3 On Mondays, my friend _____ .

4 On Saturdays, my friend doesn't _____ .

Extra Online Practice

Unit 7, Video and Grammar

Present Simple questions and short answers

?	Short answers
Do I sing?	Yes, I do. / No, I don't.
Do you sing?	Yes, you do. / No, you don't.
Does he/she/it sing?	Yes, he/she/it does. / No, he/she/it doesn't.
Do we/you/they sing?	Yes, we/you/they do. / No, we/you/they don't.

What do you do to relax?   I play computer games.

1 Circle the correct word.

1 Do / (Does) you know Mari?
2 Do / Does Tom live in a house with a garden?
3 Do / Does your friends speak English?
4 Do / Does your mum make nice cakes?
5 Do / Does I sing well?
6 Do / Does you and your sister like cats?

2 Match answers a–f to the questions in Exercise 1.

a ☐ Yes, she does.
b ☐ No, you don't.
c ☐ 1 Yes, I do.
d ☐ Yes, we do.
e ☐ No, they don't.
f ☐ Yes, he does.

3 Complete the dialogue with *do*, *does*, *don't* or *doesn't*.

Reporter: ¹___Do___ you speak any foreign languages, Superdug?
Superdug: No, I ²_____ .
Reporter: ³_____ Kit speak any foreign languages?
Superdug: Yes, she ⁴_____ .
Reporter: ⁵_____ you and Kit work together?
Superdug: Yes, we ⁶_____ .

4 Write questions.

1 you / speak Chinese?
   Do you speak Chinese?
2 you / like chocolate?
   _____
   _____
3 your teacher / ride a bike to school?
   _____
   _____
4 your friends / play football on Saturdays?
   _____
   _____
5 you / tidy your room at the weekend?
   _____
   _____
6 your dad / go to the gym?
   _____
   _____

5 Answer the questions in Exercise 4 for you.

1 _No, I don't._
2 _____
3 _____
4 _____
5 _____
6 _____

✷ 6 Complete the questions. Use *do/does* and the verbs in the box.

| do   drink   go   have   play   speak |

1 A: What __do__ you _____ after scho
   B: I usually hang out with my friends.
2 A: What _____ Sandra _____ fo
   dinner on Fridays?
   B: Pizza!
3 A: When _____ they _____ tenni
   B: At the weekend.
4 A: What _____ your pet _____ ?
   B: Water, of course.
5 A: What time _____ you _____
   to bed?
   B: At 9 o'clock.
6 A: _____ your best friend _____
   any foreign languages?
   B: Yes! My best friend is Italian!

🔊 **18 Buying a ticket**

A: Can I help you?

B: Can I have *one ticket / two tickets* to the zoo, please?

A: That's *eighteen pounds fifty*.

B: Here you are.

A: Here's your ticket. / Here are your tickets.

B: Thanks.

Read the dialogue and circle the correct answer.

A: Can I help you?

B: ¹(Can I have)/ *Would* you *like* a ticket to the museum, please?

A: ²*Would / Do* you like a guide?

B: No, ³*thanks / please.*

A: That's £8.50, please.

B: Here ⁴*are you / you are.*

A: ⁵*They're / Here are* your tickets.

B: Thank you.

Put the sentences in the dialogue in the correct order.

a ⬚ Attendant: That's £3.25, please.

b ⬚ Attendant: Thank you. And here's your sandwich.

c ⬚ 1 Attendant: Can I help you?

d ⬚ Attendant: Yes, OK. Would you like cheese in it?

e ⬚ Customer: Thanks.

f ⬚ Customer: Yes, please.

g ⬚ Customer: Here you are.

h ⬚ Customer: Yes. Can I have a sandwich, please?

LOOK! £ = pound
£4.20 = four (pounds) twenty

3 Complete the table.

1	👓	£1.50	*one pound fifty*
2	🥤	£____	two pounds fifty
3	🎟 CINEMA TICKET ADMIT ONE	£8.90	_____
4	🍿 POPCORN	£____	five pounds thirty
5	🍶	£1.20	_____

4 Complete the dialogue with one word in each gap.

A: Hello. ¹*Can* I help you?

B: Hi. Can I ² _____ two tickets for the cinema, ³ _____ ?

A: Sure. Would you ⁴ _____ a bag of popcorn?

B: ⁵ _____ , please. Good idea!

A: ⁶ _____ £15, please.

B: ⁷ _____ you are.

A: Here ⁸ _____ your tickets and ⁹ _____ 's the popcorn. Enjoy the film!

B: Thanks.

 Extra Online Practice

Unit 7, Video and Communication

All about ...
sharks

Are all sharks dangerous to people?

No, they aren't. Most sharks are not dangerous to us, but we are very dangerous to sharks! Why? Sharks don't often eat people, but in some countries people eat sharks.

So, what do sharks usually eat?

They eat fish and other sea animals. They sometimes eat other sharks.

Are they clever? What can they do?

Sharks are strong and they are fast swimmers. They can see and smell under water very well.

Can they hear?

Good question. It's amazing. They haven't got ears like ours, but they can hear fish from hundreds of kilometres away!

a shark

1 **Vocabulary** Look at the photos. Circle T (true) or F (false).

1 fast   (T)/ F

2 strong   T / F

3 dangerous T / F

4 cute   T / F

5 ugly   T / F

6 slow   T / F

2 **Which words describe sharks? Tick (✔) for *yes* and put a cross (✗) for *no*.**

dangerous ✔   fast ☐   strong ☐   lots of teeth ☐
long body ☐   cute face ☐   big ears ☐

3 **Read the text. Circle the correct answer.**

1 Sharks aren't *sometimes* /(*often*) dangerous to people.

2 People *are* / *aren't* a problem for sharks.

3 Sharks don't often eat *sea animals* / *other sharks*.

4 They *have got* / *haven't got* very good eyes.

5 They *can* / *can't* hear very well.

4 **Read the text again. Answer the questions.**

1 What do sharks usually eat?

_____

2 Do they often eat people?

_____

3 Can they smell well?

_____

4 What can they hear?

_____

1 **19 Listen to Emma and Ted. Tick (✔) the pets Emma has got.**

(A) ☐

(B) ☐

(C) ☐

19 Listen again. Answer the questions.

1 Where are the pets?
They're in Emma's bedroom.

2 Are they brothers or sisters?
_____

3 What colour is Ted's favourite pet?
_____

4 What do they need every day?
_____

5 Where does their special food come from?
_____

19 Listen again. Circle the correct answer.

1 There are _two / three_ pets.

2 Emma says they _are / aren't_ easy to look after.

3 They _like / don't like_ oranges.

4 Ted has got some _hamsters / rabbits_.

Starting and ending an email

Begin with _Hi / Hello._
Write a comma after the name, e.g. _Hi Jen, …_
Write your name at the end, e.g. _Martin._

4 Read the email. Circle the correct answer.

✉ ✕

Hi Sam,
I know you like cats. Well, our cat has got some kittens. Would you like one? They are cute. Three are black, two are black and white and one is grey. They haven't got names. They are very young!
Kittens are easy to look after. They don't go for walks! They sleep a lot and they don't eat much. They're very friendly too.
Can you ask your mum and dad? Let me know.
Ben

1 Does Sam like cats?
Yes, he does. / No, he doesn't.

2 How many kittens are there?
There are three. / There are six.

3 Have they got names?
Yes, they have. / No, they haven't.

4 Do they eat a lot?
Yes, they do. / No, they don't.

5 Can Sam have a kitten?
Yes, he can. / We don't know.

5 You have got some puppies. Write an email to a friend and offer him/her one of them. Use the words in the box or your own ideas.

black and brown
cute, funny, friendly
✔ special puppy food ✔ water ✗ milk
sleep and play

start the email	_____
describe the puppies	_____
food and drink?	_____
do?	_____
ask mum and dad?	_____
end the email	_____

Vocabulary

1 Match the word fragments to make pet words.

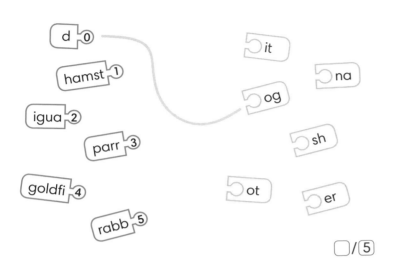

d 0
hamst 1
igua 2
parr 3
goldfi 4
rabb 5

it
na
og
sh
ot
er

☐/⑤

2 Look at the pictures. Complete the words.

0 a c<u>ute</u> c<u>a</u>t

1 a f _ _ t b _ _ d

2 a d _ _ ge _ _ us l _ _n

3 a s _ _w t _ _ to _ _ e

4 an u _ _ y f _ _g

5 a st _ _ _ g e _ _ph _ _t

☐/⑤

Grammar

3 Complete the sentences. Put the verbs in the correct form.

0 I _don't get up_ (not get up) early at weeken

1 My friend _____ (not sing) in a band.

2 We _____ (not live) in a big house.

3 Ella _____ (not like) spaghetti.

4 I _____ (not speak) French very well.

5 Mum and dad _____ (not want) a pe snake.

☐/⑤

4 Write questions. Answer yes (✔) or no (✗). Use short answers.

1 I / speak good English?

A: ⁰_Do I speak good English?_

B: ✔ ⁰⁰_Yes, you do._

2 Tom / wear jeans to school?

A: ¹_____

B: ✗ ²_____

3 your friends / like football?

A: ³_____

B: ✔ ⁴_____

4 your granny / visit you every week?

A: ⁵_____

B: ✗ No, she doesn't.

☐/⑤

Communication

5 Complete the dialogue with one word in each gap.

A: Hello, ⁰_can_ I help ¹_____ ?

B: Can I ²_____ two tickets, ³_____ ?

A: Yes, ⁴_____ fifteen pounds fifty.

B: Here you are.

A: Here ⁵_____ your tickets.

☐/

Vocabulary	☐ /⑩
Grammar	☐ /⑩
Communication	☐ /⑤
Your total score	/ 25

Extra Online Practice

Unit 7, Language Revision

Word blog: Animals

1 My photos Look at the photos. Circle the correct word.

① ② ③ ④

There is a pet shop near my school. I like it very much. There are ¹*hamsters / rabbits*, but there aren't any ²*parrots / iguanas*!
I often play with my ³*dog / cat* in the garden.
I can see lots of ⁴*butterflies / birds* in the trees!

2 My quiz Circle the correct answer.

1 Snakes	*can / can't*	run.
2 Rabbits	*eat / don't eat*	plants.
3 Tigers	*are / aren't*	dangerous.
4 Elephants	*are / aren't*	strong.
5 Kangaroos	*can / can't*	jump.
6 Butterflies	*can / can't*	swim.
7 Puppies	*are / aren't*	cute.
8 Tortoises	*are / aren't*	fast.

3 Get more Complete the sentences with the words in the box. Circle T (true) or F (false).

flies	leaves	plants	small fish	sweets

1 Lions eat _____ . T / F

2 Frogs eat _____ . T / F

3 Kangaroos eat _____ . T / F

4 Giraffes eat _____ . T / F

5 Whales eat _____ . T / F

Get more words

Amazing!

Look at the picture. Find and name eight animals.

Fun Spot

1 _____
2 _____
3 _____
4 _____
5 _____
6 _____
7 _____
8 _____

8.1 Vocabulary

1 Look at the photos. Circle the correct word.

1 (cycling) / taekwondo

2 hockey / badminton

3 sailing / windsurfing

4 basketball / volleyball

5 tennis / table tennis

6 ice-skating / roller skating

2 Look at the pictures and label the sports. Use words from Exercise 1.

1 _badminton_ 2 _____ 3 _____

4 _____ 5 _____ 6 _____

LOOK!
I do taekwondo.
I go swimming.
I play tennis.

3 Circle the correct word.

1 (go) / play ice-skating
2 do / go cycling
3 go / do taekwondo
4 play / go tennis
5 do / play football
6 go / play swimmin
7 do / go sailing
8 play / go volleyba
9 go / do skiing
10 play / do badmin

4 Match 1–6 to a–f.

1 [d] I sometimes play
2 [ ] George does
3 [ ] Do you go
4 [ ] My brother plays
5 [ ] Sandra never goes
6 [ ] Do you often play

a hockey with his friends.
b ice-skating because she can't ice-skate.
c skiing with your family?
d badminton with my dad or my brother.
e basketball at school?
f taekwondo every Monday after school.

I remem
that!

5 How many people do these sports? Put the words in the box in the right column.

skateboarding badminton basketball
hockey skiing swimming table tenis
taekwondo volleyball

👤	👥👥	👥👥👥👥👥
skateboarding		

love/like/don't like/hate + -ing

I love eating.

I don't like getting wet.

I hate cooking.

Do you like cycling? Yes, I do. / No, I don't.

What do you like doing? I like cooking.

1 Complete the sentences. Put the verbs in the correct form. Who is it? Write *Jen*, *Alex*, *Lucas* or *Lian*.

1 This person loves *playing* (play) the guitar.
Who? *Lucas*

2 This person likes _____ (make) cupcakes.
Who? _____

3 This person hates _____ (get up) early and _____ (cook).
Who? _____

4 This person likes _____ (skateboard) and _____ (climb).
Who? _____

2 Put the words in the correct order to make sentences.

1 playing Lisa the guitar loves .
Lisa loves playing the guitar.

2 does What doing like Monica ?
_____

3 going doesn't Janet like early to bed .
_____

4 films Mark watching loves funny .
_____

5 sailing and likes windsurfing Wendy .
_____

6 like Does taekwondo Tim doing ?
_____

3 Complete the sentences with the words in the box.

doesn't like	don't like	~~hate~~	hates
like	likes	love	loves

1 We ☹☹ ___hate___ rock climbing.
2 My parents ☺ _____ skiing.
3 Ann ☹☹ _____ playing football.
4 My grandad ☺☺ _____ cooking.
5 My friends ☹ _____ getting up early.
6 I ☺☺ _____ cycling.
7 Mark ☺ _____ playing basketball.
8 My cat ☹ _____ getting wet.

Object pronouns

I → me   he → him   we → us
you → you   she → her   you → you
            it → it   they → them

She is a good friend. I like her.
You don't like sports. We love them.

4 Complete the sentences with object pronouns.

1 Emma is nice. I like ___her___ .
2 Skating is fun. I love _____ .
3 You are great at football. I like watching _____ .
4 Amy and Tom are my best friends. I like _____ .
5 Tom is my baby brother. I love _____ .
6 We're good at dancing. Watch _____ !

★ 5 Complete the dialogue with the words in the box.

~~doing~~	hate	her	me	playing	plays	she

A: What does your sister like ¹*doing* at the weekend?

B: Monica is very sporty and ²_____ often goes swimming or ³_____ tennis.

A: Do you play tennis with ⁴_____ ?

B: No. I ⁵_____ it. I love ⁶_____ football! Do you want to play with ⁷_____ and my friends?

Extra Online Practice

Unit 8, Video and Grammar

71

Question words

Who is Dug's sports hero?	It's Irina Peters.
What have you got there?	I've got Irina's autograph.
When is the game?	It's on Tuesday.
Where does she live?	She lives in London.
Whose phone is it?	It's Irina's phone.
How many photos have you got?	I've got 80 photos.

1 Read the questions and circle the correct answer.

1 A: When is the football game?
   B: *It's great. /* (*It's on Saturday*).

2 A: Where is my mobile phone?
   B: *It's on the table. / It's from China.*

3 A: Whose bike is in front of the house?
   B: *The bike is green. / It's my mum's bike.*

4 A: How many friends have you got?
   B: *Five. / Five years old.*

5 A: What is in your bag?
   B: *It's next to the desk. / There's a notebook.*

6 A: Who is your English teacher?
   B: *Mr Evans is here. / It's Mr Evans.*

2 Look at the picture and circle the correct word.

1 A: (*Where*)*/ When* is Dug?
   B: He's in a shopping centre.

2 A: *Who / Whose* is the woman?
   B: She's Irina Peters.

3 A: *Who / What* is her sport?
   B: It's tennis.

4 A: *What / Who* does Dug want?
   B: He wants her autograph.

5 A: *How many / When* mobile phones can you see?
   B: Two.

3 Complete the dialogue with the words in the box.

> How many ~~What~~ When Where
> Who Whose

A: [1]*What*'s your name?

B: Marco.

A: [2]_____ are you from?

B: I'm from Italy, but I live in London now.

A: [3]_____ friends have you got in London?

B: A lot! Six or seven.

A: [4]_____ is your best friend?

B: Jacob. He's my classmate. We want to go to a party today.

A: [5]_____ party is it?

B: It's my sister's party! It's her birthday!

A: [6]_____ is the party?

B: It's at five o'clock.

✱ 4 Write questions.

1 how many classmates / you / have got?
   How many classmates have you got?

2 when / you / go to bed on Mondays?
   _____

3 where / your friends / hang out?
   _____

4 what / be / your favourite sport?
   _____

5 who / be / your favourite singer?
   _____

5 Write your answers to the questions in Exercise 4.

1 *I've got* _____ *classmates.*

2 _____

3 _____

4 _____

5 _____

🔊 20 Talking about the weather

A: What's the weather like?
B: It's *cloudy/cold/hot/rainy/snowy/sunny/ warm/windy*.
It's *cold/hot/rainy/sunny* in *winter/summer/ autumn/spring*.

Put the sentences in the dialogue in the correct order.

a ☐ Oh dear. That's horrible.
b ☐ It's cold and snowy here.
c ☐ Well, I hope it's snowy in Scotland too!
d ☐ 1 Hi, Mandy. Is the weather nice in Scotland?
e ☐ No, it isn't. It's rainy and cold!
f ☐ Yes, it's really horrible. What's the weather like in France?

Label the pictures.

sunny   2 _____   3 _____   4 _____

_____   6 _____   7 _____   8 _____

Match 1–6 to a–f.

1 ☐ c It's hot.
2 ☐ It's snowy.
3 ☐ It's windy.
4 ☐ It's rainy and wet.

a Let's go skiing.
b Let's play computer games.
c Let's go swimming.
d Let's go sailing.

4 Label the photos. Use the words in the box.

> autumn   spring   summer   winter

1 _____   2 _____

3 _____   4 _____

5 Read and circle the correct word.

What's the weather like in the UK?   QUIZ TIME

❶ It's sometimes hot in (summer) / *winter*.
❷ It's *often / never* warm in spring.
❸ It's always cold in *winter / spring*.
❹ It's often rainy and *cloudy / sunny* in autumn.
❺ It's never snowy in *winter / summer*.

6 Complete the dialogue with the words in the box.

> hope   hot   like   rainy   wet   ~~what~~

A: Hi, ¹*what*'s the weather ²_____ in New York today?
B: It's windy and ³_____ . I've got an umbrella!
A: I hate getting ⁴_____ !
B: Me too! I ⁵_____ it's sunny and ⁶_____ tomorrow.

Extra Online Practice

Unit 8, Video and Communication

73

Sam is twelve. He's very sporty. He likes getting up early but he goes to bed very late. He goes swimming before school. After school he plays football. At the weekend he goes cycling with his friends. Sam's sister Tammy is ten. She doesn't like sport and she never does exercise. She likes reading and cooking. She goes to bed at nine, and she gets up and half past six.

Sam loves cakes and chocolate and he often eats pizza and chips, but Tammy doesn't usually eat them. He doesn't like fruit and he hates vegetables – but Tammy loves them. Tammy likes chocolate but she doesn't eat it a lot. Sam usually drinks cola, but Tammy doesn't like it. She drinks fruit juice or water.

1 Read the text. Circle the correct word.

	Sam	Tammy
do exercise	often / sometimes	usually / never
eat healthy food	yes / no	yes / no

2 Read the text again. Answer the questions.

1 What exercise does Sam do in the morning?
   He goes swimming.

2 When does Tammy do exercise?
   _____

3 What does Tammy like doing?
   _____

4 What does Sam like eating?
   _____

5 Does Tammy like fruit and vegetables?
   _____

6 What does Sam usually drink?
   _____

3 **Vocabulary** Match 1–6 to a–f.

1 [d] eat   a your teeth
2 [ ] drink   b exercise
3 [ ] do   c friends
4 [ ] brush   d fruit and vegetables
5 [ ] have   e to bed early
6 [ ] go   f a lot of water

4 Look at the photos. Complete the text with expressions in Exercise 3.

I always ¹*brush* my ²_____ in the morning and after dinner. I eat a lot of ³_____ and ⁴_____ . I love apples and oranges. I ⁵_____ some ⁶_____ every week. I often go skiing or swimming. I usually ⁷_____ to ⁸_____ early, at eight.

1 Match the photos to the topics.

☐ food   ☐ sleep   ☐ exercise

A

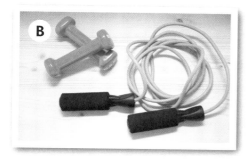

B

C

🔊 **21** Listen to the dialogue. Match the questions to the topics in Exercise 1.

Question 1: _____

Question 2: _____

Question 3: _____

🔊 **21** Listen again. Complete the notes about Tom.

Question 1

Tom's favourite food is ¹___chips___ .

He eats a lot of ²_____ and vegetables.

He drinks a lot of ³_____ .

Question 2

He likes ⁴_____ .

He always ⁵_____ to school.

He sometimes goes ⁶_____ .

Question 3

He goes to bed at ⁷_____ .

He goes to sleep at ⁸_____ .

Read through the first draft of your text to check for grammar mistakes. Check your final draft too.

I love ~~sleep~~ sleeping.

4 Read the text. Correct the underlined mistakes.

Andy ¹<u>like</u> *likes* pizza but he ²<u>don't</u> eat it very often. He ³<u>has always</u> lunch at school. He often eats a sandwich. He likes ⁴<u>read</u> and but he doesn't ⁵<u>likes</u> sport very much. His favourite sport ⁶<u>are</u> swimming. He has swimming lessons on Fridays. Andy goes to bed ⁷<u>in</u> nine because he likes ⁸<u>sleep</u>. He doesn't get up early.

5 Write about May's lifestyle. Use the information in the table.

food and drink?	fruit ☹
	vegetables ☺ ☺
	water
exercise?	walk to school / always
	do taekwondo ☺
	play badminton / at the weekend
go to bed?	10.00 / usually
get up?	7.30

May doesn't like _____

_____

_____

_____

_____

_____

_____

_____

_____

_____

_____

Check yourself!

Vocabulary

1 Circle the odd one out.

0 (roller skating) tennis football hockey
1 table tennis taekwondo badminton tennis
2 sailing windsurfing swimming ice-skating
3 spring January winter summer
4 hot warm autumn sunny
5 snowy cold windy early

☐/⑤

2 Look at the photos and complete the words.

0 do e*xercise*   **1** b_____ my teeth

2 p_____ badminton   **3** g_____ roller skating

4 d_____ a lot of water   **5** eat f_____ and vegetables

☐/⑤

Grammar

3 Write sentences.

0 Jack / hate / play / tennis
Jack hates playing tennis.
1 my sister / not like / roller skate

_____

2 you / like / swim?

_____

3 I / love / sing

_____

4 we / not like / get up / early

_____

5 your friends / like / eat / pizza?

_____

☐/⑤

4 Complete the sentences with one word in each gap.

0 A: __*Who*__ is she?
 B: She's my aunt.
1 _____ are you? Are you at school?
2 A: _____ many cookies are there?
 B: Six.
3 Your parents are nice. I like _____ .
4 Where's Emma? I can't see _____ .
5 Look at that picture! Do you like _____ ?

☐/⑤

Communication

5 Complete the dialogue with one word in each gap.

A: ⁰*What*'s the weather ¹_____ ?
B: ²_____ cold and wet.
A: Is ³_____ windy too?
B: Yes, it ⁴_____ . I hope it's sunny tomorrow.
A: ⁵_____ too!

☐/⑤

Vocabulary	☐/⑩
Grammar	☐/⑩
Communication	☐/⑤
Your total score	/ 25

Extra Online Practice

Unit 8, Language Revision

Word blog: I like that!

1 My photos What's the weather like? Circle the correct word.

1 It's *rainy / snowy*. **2** It's *sunny / cloudy*. **3** It's *cold / warm*.

2 My blog Complete the text with the words in the box.

cold   dangerous   hot   skiing   windsurfing   winter

In January and February, it's usually ¹_____ in England, but it isn't snowy. Every ²_____ we go to France because we love ³_____ .
Then, in August, we go to Spain. It's ⁴_____ there. We go swimming every day! I never go ⁵_____ . I think it's ⁶_____ .

3 Get more What are their hobbies? Complete the words.

2 w_t_r sk_ _ng

1 _m_r_c_n f_ _ tb_ll

3 h_rs_ r_d_ng

Get more words

Can I have an autograph?

What do Tina and Dale like doing? In your notebook, write six sentences.

A

B

Tina likes watching TV. Dale likes …

Fun Spot

77

Happy Families!

Jimbo, Sasha and Cheeky are our three new babies at City Zoo!

Jimbo is very strong. His ears are big and he's got a very long nose! His food is mum's milk. He loves playing in water with his friends. People at the zoo love watching him. He's friendly and he's very cute!

Sasha is a small, white baby bird. Her mum eats insects but Sasha can't eat them. She's too small. Sasha's a baby so she can't fly and she can't run. Her parents can fly and they can run … on water!

Cheeky is with mum and dad in the photo. He's small and cute. His face is pink but his parents' faces are black! He's a baby so he doesn't eat food. He drinks milk. Mum and dad can run fast and they can climb but Cheeky can't. He's too small.

Reading and Writing

1 Read the text. Circle T (true) or F (false).

0 Jimbo likes playing in water.   Ⓣ/ F
1 Jimbo is friendly.   T / F
2 Sasha's mum doesn't like insects.   T / F
3 Sasha can't run on water.   T / F
4 Cheeky's parents have got black faces.   T / F
5 Cheeky eats a lot of food.   T / F
6 Cheeky can climb.   T / F

☐/⑥

2 Look at the pictures and read the questions. Complete the answers with one word.

0 Where are the people?   in a ___*park*___
1 What's the weather like?   _____
2 What sport does the girl like? _____ skating
3 How many animals are in the picture?   _____

4 Who can run fast?   the _____
5 What has the brown dog got?   a _____
6 Where is the cat?   in the _____

☐/☐

3 Read the fact file about Jimmy's pet and answer the questions.

Pet	a parrot
Colour	yellow and blue
Food	parrot food, bananas
Abilities	can speak!
Personality	clever, funny
Likes	playing with a ball

0 What is Jimmy's pet?
It's a parrot.

1 What colour is it?
_____

2 What does it eat?
_____

3 What can it do?
_____

4 What type of personality has it got?
_____

5 What does it like doing?
_____

☐/⑤

Listening

🔊 **22** Listen and write.

Sports in my town

0 Name of sports centre:
Hillside

1 Where:
_____ the cinema

2 Number of sports:
_____

3 Team sports:
football, _____ , basketball

4 Type of food in café:
_____ food

☐/④

Communication

5 Rob's dad takes Rob and his friend Lucy to a football match. Match pictures 0–4 to sentences a–g. There are two extra sentences.

a That's fifteen pounds forty.
b Have you got your tracksuits?
c Let's go to a football match!
d Here are your coats. It's cold!
e Can I have three tickets, please?
f This game is boring.
g Can I have your autograph?

☐/④

Reading and Writing	☐/⑰
Listening	☐/④
Communication	☐/④
Your total score	/ 25

Exam Practice

Part 1 Reading and Writing

Look and read. Put a tick (✔) or a cross (✘) in the box. There are two examples.

Examples

This is a cat. ✔

This is a table. ✘

Questions

1  This is a skirt. ☐

2  This is a mountain bike. ☐

3  This is a television. ☐

4  This is a hand. ☐

5  This is a foot. ☐

Part 2 Reading and Writing

Look at the pictures. Look at the letters. Write the words.

Example

 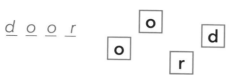

_d_ _o_ _o_ _r_

Questions

1

2

3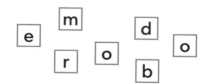

4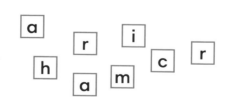

5

Part 3 Reading and Writing

Look and read. Write *yes* or *no*.

Examples

There are two boys in the room.   *yes*

There is a skateboard under the bed.   *no*

Questions

1 One of the boys has got a book.   ——————

2 There is a poster on the wall.   ——————

3 The two boys have got blond hair.   ——————

4 The ball is next to the books.   ——————

5 There is a television in front of one bed. ——————

Part 4 Listening and Communication

🔊 **23** Listen and colour. There is one example.

Part 5 Listening and Communication

Look at the pictures of children at a party in Alison's garden. Draw lines from the sentences to the pictures. Look at the pictures very carefully. There are two extra sentences.

Example

Don't worry! I'm fine!

Let me show you the bathroom.

Hold these, please.

Who's your favourite singer?

No problem.

Hi, Alison! How are you?

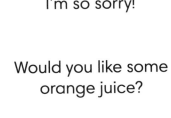

I'm so sorry!

Would you like some orange juice?

Part 1 Reading and Writing

Read this. Choose a word from the box. Write the correct word next to numbers 1–5. There is one example.

A park

My favourite place is a park. It is big with a lot of trees and _flowers_ .
¹_____ run and play here. They can ride their ²_____ and play football.

There are yellow and green ³_____ in the trees but there aren't any snakes or monkeys. There's a small ⁴_____ too. It's got great ice creams!

It opens in the ⁵_____ and it closes at six o'clock.

Example

flowers   birds   morning   school

tennis   bikes   shop   children

Part 2 Reading and Writing

Look at the pictures and read the questions. Write one-word answers. There are two examples.

Examples

How many children are there?   _five_

Where are the people?   at the   _zoo_

Questions

1 Where is the monkey?   on a   _____

What can the girls see?   a _____

Who's got the teacher's bag?   the _____

Where is the teacher now?   under the _____

What has the crocodile got?   a _____

Part 3 Listening and Communication

🔊 **24 Read the questions. Listen and write a name or a number. There are two examples.**

Examples

What is the dog's name?	_Tom_
How old is it?	_4_

Questions

1 What is the girl's name?   _____

2 What's the name of her school?   _____ House School

3 Who does she sit next to?   _____

4 How many parrots has she got?   _____

5 How many lions are in the book?   _____

Part 4 Listening and Communication

Read the text and choose the best answer.

Example

Katy: Hi! How are you?

Samuel: A I'm Samuel.

   (B) I'm fine, thanks!

   C Nice to meet you.

Questions

1 Katy: I'm hungry. Can I have a cupcake?

Samuel: A Here you are!

   B I don't like pizza.

   C I agree!

2 Katy: Where are your parents?

Samuel: A They're from Spain.

   B He's at my granny's house.

   C They're in the garden.

3 Katy: Let's do something fun!

Samuel: A He's funny.

   B No, the film isn't very funny.

   C Great idea!

4 Katy: Let's take my dog for a walk!

Samuel: A No, not again Katy!

   B I love running.

   C He doesn't like cats.

5 Katy: We can go to the cinema!

Samuel: A When does the shop open?

   B It's dangerous.

   C Let's do that!

6 Katy: How much are the tickets?

Samuel: A Have you got them?

   B Four pounds fifty.

   C There are five.

Get more on Geometry!

Shapes

1 🔊 25 **Listen and repeat. Look at the pictures and number the words in the Vocabulary box.**

Vocabulary Shapes

circle [2] line [ ] rectangle [ ]
square [ ] triangle [ ]

1 ～ 2 ● 3 ▢ 4 ▲ 5 ▬

2 **Read and match texts 1–3 to pictures A–D. There is one extra picture.**

A   B

C   D

1 [ ] Look! This is my new top. It's cool. It's blue with squares, triangles and orange and yellow lines. A small circle is on my top too.

2 [ ] My favourite top is old but it isn't boring. It's yellow with red squares, green lines and triangles. No rectangles and no circles!

3 [ ] My T-shirts are one colour. My favourite T-shirt is blue with one big rectangle, small triangles and a circle. No squares or lines!

3 **Read the texts in Exercise 2 again. Complete the table.**

	Clothes	Colours	Shapes
1	top		
2			
3			

4 **Read the sentences and circle T (true) or F (false).**

1 The rectangle on T-shirt A is small. T / F
2 T-shirt A is one colour. T / F
3 Top C is yellow with one square and one triangle. T / F
4 The squares on top C are black. T / F
5 The circle on top B is blue. T / F
6 The lines on top B are black and blue. T / F

5 **Design a T-shirt or a top with shapes. Then complete the sentences.**

This is my _____.
The shapes are _____.

Get more on Science!

Materials

1 🔊 26 Listen and repeat. Find the materials in photos 1–6.

Vocabulary Materials

cardboard   glass   metal   paper   wooden

2 Look at the picture. What is 'recycled'?

Recycled = a new thing from an old thing.

3 Look at the photos in Exercise 4 again. Which household objects are recycled?

4 Find these words in the text. Which household object is missing?

paper lamp   cardboard wardrobe
metal bath   wooden table   glass window
metal sofa

Is your house eco-friendly?

We've got a very nice house. There are many recycled household objects in it. This wooden coffee table is in our living room and it's recycled. This lamp is in my bedroom. It's my mum's idea. It's from paper. In the bathroom we've got a metal bath. It's eco-friendly but it isn't recycled. It's very old. This beautiful glass window is very old too.

My favourite object is the metal sofa in our living room. It's my dad's idea. It's grey and brown. Our house is great!

5 Read the text again. Circle *Yes* or *No*.

1 Is the house nice?   (Yes)/ No
2 Is the bath old?   Yes / No
3 Is the lamp metal?   Yes / No
4 Is the window recycled glass? Yes / No
5 Is the sofa in the bedroom?   Yes / No
6 Is the table wooden?   Yes / No

6 Think of three materials for each object.

Beds	Lamps	Doors	Desks

7 What is there in your house? Complete the sentences.

There's a/an _____ in my _____ .
It's *cardboard / glass / metal / paper / wooden*.

There are _____ in my _____ .
They're *cardboard / glass / metal / paper / wooden*.

Musical instruments

1 🔊 **27 Listen and repeat. Label photos 1–6.**

Vocabulary Musical instruments

acoustic guitar   drums   electric guitar
keyboard   melodica   violin

1 _electric guitar_

2 _____

3 _____

4 _____

5 _____

6 _____

2 Read the quiz. Circle T (true) or F (false). Check your answers on page 95. What's your score?

My score is ____ / 10

QUIZ TIME!

❶ The acoustic guitar is from France.	T / F
❷ The guitar has got a head, a neck and a body.	T / F
❸ When you play the guitar, its head is on your legs.	T / F
❹ You play the melodica with your mouth and toes.	T / F
❺ You play the drums with your fingers and feet.	T / F
❻ The violin is a glass instrument.	T / F
❼ The keyboard is an electric instrument.	T / F
❽ The body of the electric guitar is usually wooden.	T / F
❾ The violin and the acoustic guitar are in the same family of instruments.	T / F
❿ The drums are from the USA.	T / F

3 Look at the false sentences in the quiz. Correct them using the words in the bo

body   China   fingers   ~~Spain~~   woo

1 The acoustic guitar is from _Spain_
2 When you play the guitar, its _____ on your legs.
3 You play the melodica with your mout and _____ .
4 The violin is a _____ instrument.
5 The drums are from _____ .

4 What can Jane play? Look at the quiz again. Read and complete the text.

My name's Jane. I can play the _____ It's wooden and it's big. You play this instrument with your fingers. And I love i colours: brown and black.

5 Imagine you can play one of the instruments from the quiz and complet Use Exercise 4 to help.

I can play the _____ . It's _____ and _____ . You play this instrument with your _____ .

Get more on Sports!
Sports equipment

1 🔊 28 **Listen and repeat. Find these objects in the photos in Exercise 2.**

Vocabulary Sports equipment

bat ☐ goggles ☐ helmet ☐ net ☐ racket ☐ stick ☐

2 **What sports do these teens like? Complete the texts with the words in the box. There are four extra sports.**

> badminton cycling football hockey roller skating
> table tennis tennis swimming volleyball

1 I love _____ because I can hang out with my friends outside and be active. We ride our bikes at the weekend. I always wear a helmet.

a

2 I like _____ . I play on Saturdays with my brother. You need a small ball and a bat for this sport. You play the ball on a table with a net. There are usually two or four players.

b

c

4 I like _____ . I'm in a club. I train every day and I think I'm good at it. I wear goggles because I hate getting water in my eyes. I wear a swimming cap too because I've got long hair.

d

3 **Look at the texts again and underline four more pieces of equipment.**

4 **Complete the table with equipment words from the texts.**

Tennis	
Hockey	
Volleyball	
Football	
Swimming	
Table tennis	
Cycling	

5 **Do you like sport? Complete the sentences for you.**

I like _____ . I *play / go / do* _____ with _____ .
To do this sport I need _____ .

3 I love playing _____ . I often play with my sister. We play on Wednesdays and Fridays. I have a new racket. It's a birthday present.

e

5 I love _____ . I like playing on ice but you can play this sport on grass too. You need a long stick to play. And it's also good to wear a helmet.

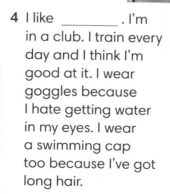

f

Answer key

Get started! Check yourself!

Exercise 1

1 sixty 2 thirty-two 3 blue 4 yellow 5 black

Exercise 2

1 pencil case 2 notebook 3 chair 4 sandwich 5 clock

Exercise 3

1 They're 2 a 3 It's 4 an 5 They're

Exercise 4

1 oranges 2 boxes 3 bins 4 umbrellas 5 rubbers

Exercise 5

1 please 2 down 3 books 4 pairs 5 up

1.7 Check yourself!

Exercise 1

1 aunt 2 father 3 brother 4 daughter 5 granny

Exercise 2

1 garden 2 American 3 school 4 France 5 home

Exercise 3

1 are 2 is/'s 3 are not / aren't 4 are/'re 5 am not / 'm not

Exercise 4

1 His 2 Freddie's 3 her 4 Nadia's 5 Clara's

Exercise 5

1 is 2 Hi/Hello 3 Nice 4 meet 5 too

2.7 Check yourself!

Exercise 1

1 boring 2 backpack 3 cap 4 top 5 skirt

Exercise 2

1 mobile phone 2 shirt 3 jeans/trousers 4 trainers/shoes
  5 skateboard

Exercise 3

1 a 2 b 3 b 4 a 5 b

Exercise 4

1 Yes, it is. 2 No, they aren't. 3 Yes, we are. 4 No, he isn't.
  5 Yes, she is.

Exercise 5

a 3 b 5 d 1 e 2 f 4

Skills Revision 1&2

Exercise 1

b

Exercise 2

1 cake 2 friends 3 isn't 4 are 5 new 6 top

Exercise 3

1 no 2 no 3 yes 4 no 5 yes

Exercise 4

1 is from the UK / is British 2 is 11/eleven (years old) 3 is
  Katia 4 are purple and white 5 is her jacket

Exercise 5

1 C 2 B 3 C 4 A

Exercise 6

1 f 2 e 3 a 4 b

3.7 Check yourself!

Exercise 1

1 armchair 2 wardrobe 3 window 4 cushion 5 table

Exercise 2

1 bedroom 2 under 3 kitchen 4 in front of 5 fridge

Exercise 3

1 are 2 a pen 3 aren't 4 is 5 aren't

Exercise 4

1 isn't 2 Are 3 any 4 aren't 5 a

Exercise 5

a 4 b 3 c 5 e 1 f 2

4.7 Check yourself!

Exercise 1

1 long 2 big 3 nose 4 legs 5 helpful

Exercise 2

1 long 2 straight 3 curly 4 friendly 5 clever

Exercise 3

1 Has 2 got 3 Have 4 haven't 5 hasn't

Exercise 4

1 Their 2 your 3 Its 4 Our 5 its

Exercise 5

1 problem 2 mistake 3 all right 4 you OK 5 I'm fine

Skills Revision 3&4

Exercise 1

1 F 2 T 3 F 4 T 5 F

Exercise 2

1 are 2 sister 3 kitchen 4 small 5 got 6 old 7 behind

Exercise 3

1 He's American. / He's from the USA.
2 He's got short brown hair.
3 He's got blue eyes.
4 He's friendly and funny.
5 He's got two sisters.

Exercise 4

1 A 2 B 3 A 4 C

Exercise 5

1 c 2 e 3 a 4 g

5.7 Check yourself!

Exercise 1

1 jump 2 write 3 climb 4 cook 5 skateboard

Exercise 2

1 play 2 make 3 read 4 ride 5 play

Exercise 3

1 can 2 and 3 but 4 can't 5 can

Exercise 4
1 Yes, she can.
2 Can the dogs sing?
3 No, they can't.
4 Can the boy ride his bike?
5 Yes, he can.

Exercise 5
1 can 2 sure 3 can't 4 problem 5 Great/Good

6.7 Check yourself!

Exercise 1
1 have 2 hang 3 play 4 watch 5 go

Exercise 2
1 August 2 Saturday 3 November 4 April 5 Wednesday

Exercise 3
1 go 2 likes 3 tidies 4 do 5 have

Exercise 4
1 I am always busy.
2 We often play tennis.
3 Mum never watches TV.
4 I sometimes tidy my room.
5 Jess is usually late.

Exercise 5
1 past 2 is 3 minutes 4 at 4 clock

Skills Revision 5&6

Exercise 1
a

Exercise 2
1 T 2 T 3 F 4 F 5 T 6 F

Exercise 3
1 pancakes 2 homework 3 bedroom 4 television
5 friends

Exercise 4
1 She has breakfast at eight (o'clock).
2 She goes to school at half past eight.
3 She has lessons all day!
4 She does her homework at five (o'clock).
5 She has dinner at granny's house at quarter to seven.

Exercise 5
1 E 2 A 3 C 4 B

Exercise 6
1 C 2 B 3 A 4 A

7.7 Check yourself!

Exercise 1
1 hamster 2 iguana 3 parrot 4 goldfish 5 rabbit

Exercise 2
1 a fast bird 2 a dangerous lion 3 a slow tortoise
4 an ugly frog 5 a strong elephant

Exercise 3
1 doesn't sing 2 don't live 3 doesn't like 4 don't speak
5 don't want

Exercise 4
1 Does Tom wear jeans to school?
2 No, he doesn't.
3 Do your friends like football?
4 Yes, they do.
5 Does your granny visit you every week?

Exercise 5
1 you 2 have 3 please 4 that's 5 are

8.7 Check yourself!

Exercise 1
1 taekwondo 2 ice-skating 3 January 4 autumn 5 early

Exercise 2
1 brush 2 play 3 go 4 drink 5 fruit

Exercise 3
1 My sister doesn't like roller skating.
2 Do you like swimming?
3 I love singing.
4 We don't like getting up early.
5 Do your friends like eating pizza?

Exercise 4
1 Where 2 How 3 them 4 her 5 it

Exercise 5
1 like 2 It's 3 it 4 is 5 Me

Skills Revision 7&8

Exercise 1
1 T 2 F 3 T 4 T 5 F 6 F

Exercise 2
1 sunny 2 roller 3 three 4 man 5 sandwich 6 tree

Exercise 3
1 It's yellow and blue.
2 It eats parrot food and bananas.
3 It can speak!
4 It's clever and funny.
5 It likes playing with a ball.

Exercise 4
1 next to 2 15/fifteen 3 volleyball 4 healthy

Exercise 5
1 d 2 e 3 a 4 g

Get more on Music!

Page 92, Exercise 2
1 F 2 T 3 F 4 F 5 T 6 F 7 T 8 T 9 T 10 F